C0-AUY-780

VIEW
POINTS

VIEW POINTS

Perspectives of Faith and Christian Nurture

H. Edward Everding Jr.
Mary M. Wilcox
Lucinda A. Huffaker
Clarence H. Snelling Jr.

TRINITY PRESS INTERNATIONAL
Harrisburg, Pennsylvania

BT
771.2
.V54
1998

Copyright © 1998 by H. Edward Everding Jr., Mary M. Wilcox, Lucinda A. Huffaker, Clarence H. Snelling Jr.

All rights reserved. No part of this book may be reproduced, stored in a re-trieval system, or transmitted, in any form or by any means, electronic, mechanical, photocopying, recording, or otherwise, without the written permission of the publisher.

Trinity Press International, P.O. Box 1321, Harrisburg, PA 17105
Trinity Press International is part of the Morehouse Group

Library of Congress Cataloging-in-Publication Data
Everding, H. Edward.
    Viewpoints : perspectives of faith and Christian nurture / H. Edward Everding, Jr. ... [et al.].
        p.   cm.
    Includes bibliographical references and index.
    ISBN 1-56338-222-9 (alk. paper)
    1. Faith development. 2. Faith – Psychology. 3. Christian education – Philosophy. 4. Moral development. 5. Christianity – Psychology. 6. Developmental psychology. 7. Bible – Study and teaching.   I. Title.
BT771.2.E84 1998
234'.23–dc21   97-45508
                                                         CIP

Printed in the United States of America

98   99   00   01   02   10   9   8   7   6   5   4   3   2   1

Contents

Preface

Viewpoints! How and why are they formed? What causes people to think certain things and to hold different points of view? These simple, intriguing questions form the roots of the authors' shared interest in the forms and contents of individuals' thinking in various life situations. The research and its applications that gave birth to this book grew out of our passion to understand why people differ and how those individual differences shape their expressions of faith.

This cooperative venture draws on the rich resources of each contributing author's particular journey to arrive at a common concern for how the church and society deal with diversity. As a child growing up in the South and later as a southern pastor, Clarence experienced the dissonance of people's ways of thinking about race relations and civil rights. He felt it imperative to understand and communicate with those whose differing perspectives and positions caused escalating conflict. Educated as a geologist, Mary used her abilities to analyze rock formations to develop her own ways of thinking and communicating about Christian faith. When discussions and educational experiences in the church led her to graduate theological education, she was frustrated when some of the instruction there did not challenge her to think or did not respect what and how she thought.

While still a child in elementary school, Ed was often perplexed by his dad's challenges to think critically. In graduate school, he related those early experiences to biblical hermeneutics, or how persons come to understand a text and themselves in relation to the text. Lucinda's interest in developmental psychology led to her fascination with the shape of persons' faith journeys. Her teaching and participation in the local church exposed her to intriguing differences among people's religious faith and its expression in beliefs, ritual, and individual piety. Finally, and not incidentally, each of us can attest to the profound impact on our journeys of hours spent with our fledgling philosopher-children, exploring their ideas on issues such as conscientious objection and Christian faith and trying to answer their questions ("Is the Bible true?") in honest and understandable ways.

What were at first our individual and idiosyncratic interests in persons' ways of thinking became interconnected through our respective formal entrances into the field of cognitive developmental research. Clarence's interdisciplinary study of the forms of language led to a sabbatical leave and postdoctoral study in 1970 with Jean Piaget and Bärbel Inhelder at

the Graduate School of Education, University of Geneva.[1] Mary's graduate studies under Clarence at the Iliff School of Theology introduced her to
Piaget's theory of development in logical thinking. Her chance reading of
an article about Lawrence Kohlberg's theory of development in moral reasoning led to the inclusion of Kohlberg's work, particularly his concept of
social perspective, in teaching and research methodology. She in turn introduced Ed to Piaget's and Kohlberg's work when they team-taught a course
called "Teaching the Bible in the Local Church." This chain of involvement continued with Lucinda, whose study and later team-teaching with
Ed helped her expand the dialogue between gender issues and the cognitive
developmental model. Ed's background in New Testament studies enabled
him to link creatively Piaget's and Kohlberg's research and styles of biblical
interpretation. This led to initial explorations with children and their ways
of thinking about parables.[2] A sabbatical leave provided an opportunity for
Ed to learn more about work being conducted at Harvard by Kohlberg on
moral reasoning, James W. Fowler on faith development, and William G.
Perry Jr. on intellectual and ethical development. The framework created
by their research, combined with our own explorations into interpretation
and development, provided the structure for a longitudinal research project
on adults' interpretations of religious symbols, authority, the Bible, and the
plurality of truth claims.[3]

Although this research formed an initial empirical foundation for this
book, it has been the succeeding years of drawing insights from the research
and applying, testing, and adapting it in actual settings that have generated
what we believe to be a significant contribution to the understanding of
adult faith and Christian nurture.[4] The amplification of our initial discov-

---

1. The evolution of Snelling's work on language and faith can be found in "The Teaching
Ministry: Four Types of Language," *Iliff Review* (spring 1966): 33–40; "Symbolic Formation:
A Structural-Developmental Study of Religious Language as Used by Theological Students"
(presidential address given to the Association of Professors and Researchers in Religious Edu-
cation, Hartford, Conn., October 1978); and his commencement address delivered at the Iliff
School of Theology graduation ceremony in Denver, on May 28, 1993.

2. See H. Edward Everding Jr., "Implications of Jean Piaget's Theory of Cognitive Development for Teaching the Bible: A Programmatic Essay" (paper presented at the annual meeting
of the Society of Biblical Literature, Washington, D.C., October 1974); and H. Edward
Everding Jr. and Mary M. Wilcox, "Implications of Kohlberg's Theory of Moral Reasoning for Biblical Interpretation" (paper presented at the annual meeting of the Association of
Professors and Researchers in Religious Education, Philadelphia, November 1975).

3. The research project was supported by the Association of Theological Schools, the Andrew W. Mellon Foundation, the Arthur Vining Davis Foundation, and the Iliff School of
Theology. A report of this research, conducted with Iliff students from 1977 to 1983, can be
found in appendix B.

4. See, for example, Everding, "Implications of Jean Piaget's Theory"; Mary M. Wilcox
and H. Edward Everding Jr., "The Boss Doesn't Get in Trouble," *JED SHARE* (August 1975):
5–6; Everding and Wilcox, "Implications of Kohlberg's Theory"; H. Edward Everding Jr.,
Clarence H. Snelling Jr., and Mary M. Wilcox, "Toward a Theory of Instruction for Religious Education" (paper presented at the annual meeting of the Association of Professors
and Researchers in Religious Education, Toronto, Ont., November 1976); Mary M. Wilcox,

eries has included developing applications for various groups and topics, testing the theory's adequacy across cultures, shaping curriculum and experimenting with teaching strategies congruent with its implications, and including new material as it became available. Over the years, one major consequence has continually emerged in our research, study, preaching, teaching, and training. We have discovered that providing this kind of information about how people think in different ways helps them better understand and communicate with each other. Individual contributions to this book converge in our shared commitment to new visions of community that respect differences and generate trust and solidarity. Whether the issues concern conflict resolution, human sexuality, ordination criteria, or justice and peace, human understanding is our bridge to a hopeful future together.

H. Edward Everding Jr., and Clarence H. Snelling Jr., "Interpretation and Truth in Adult Development" (paper presented at the annual meeting of the Association of Professors and Researchers in Religious Education, Toronto, Ont., November 1979); and Mary M. Wilcox, *Developmental Journey: A Guide to the Development of Logical and Moral Reasoning and Social Perspective* (Nashville: Abingdon, 1979).

Acknowledgments

This book had its origin a generation ago, in 1977, and could never have come to fruition without the contributions and assistance of numerous persons. Many of those people were students at the Iliff School of Theology, including the 179 student subjects who were interviewed one or more times; the 30 student members of the research team who helped conduct and score the 252 interviews; and the student members of the research seminars who did follow-up verification and analysis. We also express our appreciation to the people who transcribed the interviews, especially Elinor Lewallen, who worked with us faithfully over a period of several years, and to Ray E. Wilcox and Karyn Kruse for statistical runs on scores.

The research project was supported by the Association of Theological Schools, the Andrew W. Mellon Foundation, and the Arthur Vining Davis Foundation. We particularly acknowledge the contributions of the Iliff School of Theology, which provided the setting for the research and for the classes that stimulated our thinking and our creativity. Iliff also supported the Development and Education Center, the administrative structure through which we implemented our research and teaching over the years.

At the beginning of our project, in 1977, we received excellent instruction in interviewing and scoring moral dilemma interviews by members of the Center for Moral Education at the Graduate School of Education, Harvard University. We are especially indebted to Anne Colby and Robert Kegan for their assistance at that time.

Numerous colleagues in the Association for Professors and Researchers in Religious Education gave us their encouragement and support throughout the period of our research and reporting at various annual meetings of this professional society.

Finally, we offer our thanks to Harold W. Rast, publisher, and Laura Barrett, managing editor, at Trinity Press International for their interest and guidance.

INTRODUCTION

Perspective is a wonderful word that reminds us both of expanding our vision and that, as vantage points change, so does our vision. There are many perspectives, and a lot of life is in the seeing.

—David Houston[1]

Diversity is a fact of our existence. Although scientists learn daily more and more about the interconnectedness, interdependence, and evolving ordered complexity of all that is in the universe, they also assure us that these connections do not dictate uniformity. Hence, there is no single "perfect bird," but a multitude of species within which no two creatures are identical. A simple pattern for "birdness" produces an infinite number of possibilities. Evolutionary ecologist Sally Goerner reminds us that "difference is the seed of change and growth."[2] As varieties of plants and animals disappear from our planet, we are becoming more aware of the beauty and richness of experience that diversity provides. Creative possibilities multiply exponentially as interactive groups increase in heterogeneity.

However, it is obvious that diversity is not only a gift to be enjoyed, it is also a problem to be solved. Difference can be threatening or confusing. It might mean the displacement or destruction of the familiar. It can lead to disunity and chaos. In our human world, we are well acquainted with both the creative potential and the uncomfortable discord inherent in the phenomenon of difference. When we are confronted by others who look different, behave differently, or believe differently, our responses can be any mixture of fascination, mistrust, and acceptance. Some people will exclude or ignore different people or differing opinions; others might assimilate, integrate, ridicule, co-opt, or destroy them.

In the midst of such diversity, the church works to bring people together in communities that affirm the dignity and worth of all persons. At the same time, these communities are called to live out their particular Christian values in and for the world, bearing witness to God's realm on earth. How can we understand and work constructively with the diversity of viewpoints, experiences, values, and abilities we see in people every day?

---

1. The Sunday "Announcements" of Saint John's Episcopal Cathedral, Denver, Colo., second Sunday after Epiphany, January 14, 1996.
2. Sally J. Goerner, *Chaos and the Evolving Ecological Universe* (Amsterdam: Gordon & Breach, 1994), 153.

1

How can we agree with one another about a vision to which God calls us? How can we work together even though we disagree? This book represents our evolving responses to those questions.

Difference and Perspective

One way of attending to the differences among people is to consider different perspectives, or ways of looking at or thinking about the world. We know that things look different when we see them from different locations. Objects appear larger when we are close to them than they do when we move farther away. Things appear to be shaped differently if one looks down on them rather than looking at them from the side. "Points of view" can also describe opinions people hold or particular ways they interpret a series of events (e.g., points of view about who was at fault in an automobile accident). "Social location" explains some very different views of our nation's economy, based on whether one grew up in an urban ghetto or a high-priced suburb.

In this book, we are concerned with the diversity created by persons' different viewpoints, or their perspectives. After an introduction to the concept of different perspectives in a local church workshop, one participant wrote the following:

> *Perspective* is a wonderful word that reminds us both of expanding our vision and that, as vantage points change, so does our vision. There are many perspectives, and a lot of life is in the seeing. As psychotherapist Albert Ellis says, nothing that happens to you is as important as how you see it. What are we looking for? It may be close at hand, still moving us into a deep intensity for a time.[3]

Because there are different perspectives, something known from only one perspective is only partially known! The apostle Paul articulated his understanding of difference and the ultimate partiality of our knowing in his letter to persons who prophesied and spoke in tongues in congregational meetings at Corinth:

> Love never ends. But as for prophecies, they will come to an end; as for tongues, they will cease; as for knowledge, it will come to an end. For we know only in part, and we prophesy only in part; but when the complete comes, the partial will come to an end. When I was a child, I spoke like a child, I thought like a child, I reasoned like a child; when I became an adult, I put an end to childish ways. For now we see in a mirror, dimly, but then we will see face to face. Now I know only in part; then I will know fully, even as I have been

---

3. Sunday "Announcements," Saint John's Episcopal Cathedral.

fully known. And now faith, hope, and love abide, these three; and the greatest of these is love. (1 Cor. 13:8–13 NRSV)

An awareness that our knowledge is incomplete and imperfect opens the way for us to be more receptive to different ideas and ways of thinking about our worlds of meaning. It provides a foundation for empathy, loving acceptance, and a basis for dealing with conflict.

Perspectives and Cognition

Our exploration of different perspectives held by adults focuses on cognitive structures that shape how persons interpret concepts and experiences. In particular, our research has roots in the cognitive structural developmental theories and research that have evolved from the work of Jean Piaget.[4] Central concepts of these theories include cognition, structure, and development. *Cognition* refers to the mental process of thinking, reasoning, knowing, and composing meaning or interpreting. *Structure* pertains to the innate patterning process of the brain, which has the capacity to increase its complexity when the individual interacts with the environment. *Development* involves the potential sequential and irreversible transformations of these structures, resulting in expressions of different perspectives or ways of thinking about concepts and issues.

Our research and experience build upon and contribute to these theories in five ways. First, because the subjects of our research were adults who demonstrated capacity for formal operations, our work expands and elaborates the description of adult perspectives. Second, we explore the expressions of different adult perspectives through persons' styles of interpreting the Bible and their ways of thinking about the authority of the Bible, tradition, images of the Bible, truth, and themselves as interpreters. Third, we describe examples of what William Perry identified as multiplistic thinking and suggest that this way of thinking constitutes a distinct perspective in its own right.[5] Fourth, we formulate interpretations of various concepts (e.g., church, prayer, teacher, learner), based on composites drawn

---

4. For examples of cognitive structural developmental theory and research, see Bärbel Inhelder and Jean Piaget, *The Growth of Logical Thinking from Childhood to Adolescence* (New York: Basic Books, 1969); Mary Ann Spencer Pulaski, *Understanding Piaget: An Introduction to Children's Cognitive Development* (New York: Harper, 1971); William G. Perry Jr., *Forms of Intellectual and Ethical Development in the College Years* (New York: Holt, Rinehart & Winston, 1970); James W. Fowler, *Stages of Faith: The Psychology of Human Development and the Quest for Meaning* (San Francisco: Harper & Row, 1981); Lawrence Kohlberg, *Essays on Moral Development*, 2 vols. (San Francisco: Harper & Row, 1981, 1984); Mary Field Belenky et al., *Women's Ways of Knowing: The Development of Self, Voice, and Mind* (New York: Basic Books, 1986); and Mary M. Wilcox, *Developmental Journey: A Guide to the Development of Logical and Moral Reasoning and Social Perspective* (Nashville: Abingdon, 1979).

5. Perry, *Forms of Intellectual and Ethical Development*, 72–108. This perspective, which we have labeled "B," corresponds to Stage $3\frac{1}{2}$ in Kohlberg's theory of moral reasoning and to

from actual interviews, to suggest how understanding the different perspectives might assist persons engaged in ministry. Fifth, we offer concrete and practical suggestions for using this perspectival theory to address issues of diversity in the practice of Christian nurture.

To this end, the book proceeds from description to applications, maintaining its practical integrity by citing individual interviews and by anchoring theory in educational strategies. Chapter 1 introduces the concept of perspectives of faith and clarifies our usage of "faith" and "nurture." Chapters 2 through 6 describe four adult perspectives of faith based on our research and other theories of cognitive development. Chapter 7 illustrates how this information can contribute to the teaching-learning process. Chapters 8 through 12 explore implications and present applications of perspectival theory for the practice of religious nurture. The final chapter concludes by reflecting on the impact of diversity — such as the diversity created by perspectives of faith — on our efforts to create community and to increase understanding within the human family.

Patterns of thinking provide one way of examining differences among people. However, the human person is an amazingly complex and integrated phenomenon, the beauty and mystery of which cannot be described by any single theory of development. Our use of theories of cognition is not intended to be reductionist. (After all, as we have seen, the partiality of our own knowledge is a fundamental premise of theories themselves!) Cognition is only one attribute of this highly complex organism, and thinking is too complex to be explained by the language of one scientific system. Deepak Chopra has said it well in his book *Quantum Healing*: "To think is to form patterns inside ourselves that are just as complex, fleeting, and rich in their diversity as is reality itself. Thinking is the mirror of the world and nothing less. Science simply does not have the tools to look at such a phenomenon, which is at once infinite and alive."[6]

Rather than claim an unrealistic comprehensiveness, we would like this book to stand with others that explore how humans create meaning by trying to understand themselves and their worlds. Human constructions of what is real are shaped by and reflected in alternative scientific paradigms, multisensory consciousness, social and gendered constructions of reality, the universal energy field, and models of the mind.[7] Chopra reminds us

---

"young adult faith" in Sharon Parks, *The Critical Years: The Young Adult Search for a Faith to Live By* (San Francisco: Harper & Row, 1986).

6. Deepak Chopra, *Quantum Healing: Exploring the Frontiers of Mind/Body Medicine* (New York: Bantam, 1989), 50.

7. On alternate scientific paradigms, see Thomas S. Kuhn, *The Structure of Scientific Revolutions*, 2d ed. (Chicago: University of Chicago Press, 1970); Marilyn Ferguson, *The Aquarian Conspiracy: Personal and Social Transformation in the 1980s* (Los Angeles: Tarcher, 1980); Fritjof Capra, *The Turning Point: Science, Society, and the Rising Culture* (New York: Bantam, 1983); and Michael Talbot, *The Holographic Universe* (New York: HarperPerennial, 1991). On multisensory consciousness, see Joel S. Goldsmith, *Consciousness Unfolding* (Secaucus,

that scientific "models are useful, but without exception they have blind spots built into them."[8] It is the blind spots that either cripple our attempts to "know fully" or motivate us to produce more accurate and adequate renditions of our human experience. This book offers our contribution to understanding different perspectives of faith and how they can be nurtured.

N.J.: Citadel, 1962); Gary Zukav, *The Seat of the Soul* (New York: Simon & Schuster, 1989); and Larry Dossey, *Recovering the Soul: A Scientific and Spiritual Search* (New York: Bantam, 1989). On social and gendered constructions of reality, see Peter L. Berger and Thomas Luckman, *The Social Construction of Reality: A Treatise in the Sociology of Knowledge* (Garden City, N.Y.: Doubleday, 1966); Walter Truett Anderson, *Reality Isn't What It Used to Be: Theatrical Politics, Ready-to-Wear Religion, Global Myths, Primitive Chic, and Other Wonders of the Postmodern World* (San Francisco: Harper, 1990); Elizabeth Kamarck Minnich, *Transforming Knowledge* (Philadelphia: Temple University Press, 1990); and Belenky et al., *Women's Ways of Knowing*. On the universal energy field, see Barbara Ann Brennan, *Hands of Light: A Guide to Healing through the Human Energy Field* (New York: Bantam, 1987). On models of the mind, see Paul Watzlawick, *The Invented Reality: How Do We Know What We Believe We Know? Contributions to Constructivism* (New York: Norton, 1984); and Jerome Brunner, *Actual Minds, Possible Worlds* (Cambridge: Harvard University Press, 1986).

    8. Chopra, *Quantum Healing*, 55.

Part 1

Viewpoints: Four Adult Faith Perspectives

THE FOLLOWING CHAPTERS introduce the concept of perspectives of faith and present profiles of four adult perspectives by describing how each thinks about six topics related to the Bible. Quotations representing these faith perspectives come from individuals who responded to questions in our Biblical Interview based on the following text:

> But as for you, continue in what you have learned and have firmly believed, knowing from whom you learned it and how from childhood you have been acquainted with the sacred writings which are able to instruct you for salvation through faith in Christ Jesus. All scripture is inspired by God and profitable for teaching, for reproof, for correction, and for training in righteousness, that the man of God may be complete, equipped for every good work. (2 Tim. 3:14–17 RSV)

The Biblical Interview was designed to probe thinking about (1) how one interprets a biblical text, (2) the authority of the Bible, (3) tradition, (4) images of the Bible, (5) truth, and (6) one's self-understanding as an interpreter (see appendix B). Illustrative quotations from our research not only fill out the picture of each perspective but also reveal how one's struggle between viewpoints or perspectives often characterizes the dynamic process we've called faith. We conclude this discussion by demonstrating how an understanding of adult faith perspectives can enrich an educational experience through sensitive consideration of the variety of ways that individuals will think about that experience.

1

PERSPECTIVES OF FAITH

Faith is a dynamic, composing, multi-faceted activity.
— Sharon Parks[1]

When we asked persons in various class and church settings to respond to the question "What does faith mean to you?" they answered in ways that represent the rich diversity through which faith has been understood throughout history (e.g., trust, action, belief, risk, sensation, and feeling).[2] Overall, their responses seem to fall into two categories. Some understand faith rather specifically, as faith in God (e.g., "partnership with God," "I'll take things as far as I can and trust God will take it from there"). Others understand faith in a more general way, as something like a human capacity or disposition (e.g., "meaning making," "confidence," "seeing past appearances," "strength to believe in impossible situations," "to let go").

In our experience we have found it more meaningful to conceptualize faith as a dynamic process through which persons make sense out of the experiences of their lives.[3] Faith involves *centers* of loyalty, values, and ultimate concerns: "For where your treasure is, there your heart will be also" (Matt. 6:21 NRSV). Faith also involves *ways of knowing and expressing* those centers that display persons' dispositions toward life and their ways of being in the world. *Perspectives of faith* (modes of cognition, including perception, thinking, reasoning, and understanding) constitute *one* way by which those centers are known and expressed: "I understand and believe that..." Other expressions include the following:

---

1. Sharon Parks, *Critical Years*, 26.
2. For a historical perspective on the meanings of faith, see the collection *Handbook of Faith*, edited by James Michael Lee (Birmingham, Ala.: Religious Education Press, 1990).
3. This definition of faith differs from faith as belief in a particular body of doctrine (e.g., the "sound doctrine" in the Pastoral Epistles) or as a right relationship with God or a gift of God (see, e.g., Richard Robert Osmer, *Teaching for Faith* [Louisville, Ky.: Westminster/John Knox, 1992], 16). Our use of "faith" more closely approximates the discussion of "human faith" as a holistic process of interpretation by Fowler, *Stages of Faith;* and Parks, *Critical Years*, 9–27.

Action: "I by my works will show you my faith."
   (Behavior, response, obedience to moral imperatives, lifestyle, faith-fulness)

Affect: "I feel I can trust you."
   (Subjective feeling, emotional experience, personal trust, confidence)

Imagination: "I picture God as a friend and helper I can trust."
   (Imagining, forming mental images and pictures)

Intuition: "I am aware of your presence."
   (Immediate perception and apprehension, synchronicity, independent of reasoning)

Sensation: "I am embraced by Jesus' touch and see his love in your face."
   (Sensory knowing)

Volition: "I have decided to act more lovingly."
   (Willing, choosing, resolving, deciding, committing, orienting life)

Perspectives (modes of cognition): "I understand and believe that . . . "
   (Perception, thinking, reasoning, understanding)

Figure 1 illustrates the interplay of centers and expressions of faith as a dynamic process. Different expressions of faith might be more prevalent at certain times or with certain personalities or groups of people. It is the ebb and flow of different types of expressions out of centers of ultimate concern — which also shift and change as we move through life — that create the dynamic process we call faith.

Perspectives of Faith and Developmental Theory

We have chosen to focus our attention on the cognitive ways of knowing and expressing faith's centers (i.e., perspectives of faith) for two reasons. First, more than twenty-five years of teaching, research, and writing about structural developmental theories have convinced us that persons' cognitive structures constitute an important reason why people see the world differently. These structures shape the patterns and meanings that persons construct out of their experiences by assimilating information into characteristic modes of interpretation. Although we ground this confidence on data from our and others' research, it is the second reason that is most compelling, and that is the confirmation of the theory's usefulness by persons who have participated in our classes and workshops. Learning about the different perspectives has contributed to self-awareness, communication skills, understanding of people's diverse patterns of thinking, and growth in their own ways of composing meaning.

   The close association between language and perspectives contributes to the power of the latter as a way of knowing and expressing faith. As the

Faith Expressions

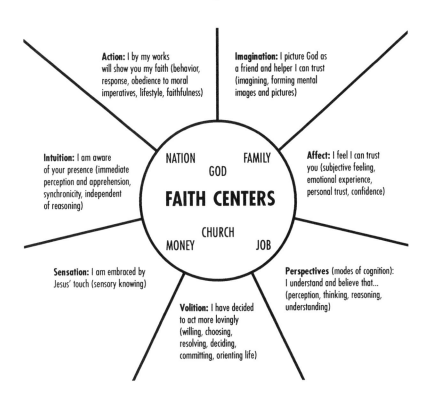

Action: I by my works will show you my faith (behavior, response, obedience to moral imperatives, lifestyle, faithfulness)

Imagination: I picture God as a friend and helper I can trust (imagining, forming mental images and pictures)

Intuition: I am aware of your presence (immediate perception and apprehension, synchronicity, independent of reasoning)

Affect: I feel I can trust you (subjective feeling, emotional experience, personal trust, confidence)

NATION   FAMILY
GOD
FAITH CENTERS
CHURCH
MONEY   JOB

Sensation: I am embraced by Jesus' touch (sensory knowing)

Perspectives (modes of cognition): I understand and believe that... (perception, thinking, reasoning, understanding)

Volition: I have decided to act more lovingly (willing, choosing, resolving, deciding, committing, orienting life)

Figure 1

major vehicle of communication, language conveys our faith to others, and cognition coordinates and integrates our various experiences of faith into language. Language inevitably reduces the totality of our experience, because the brain must select and organize portions of experience into meaningful expression through words and syntax. Hence, once again, we are confronted with the partiality of our knowledge — this time because it is inevitably reduced as it is communicated through language. Perspectives of faith, although being only one of the modes of knowing and expressing faith's centers, open an important window on the dynamics of faith and diversity, because language is the vehicle for expressing, analyzing, and negotiating differences.

Structural developmental theory traces the transformations of cognitive structures through their potential stages of increasingly ordered complexity.[4] The process of development is characterized by the following:

1. Theoretically, all persons' reasoning capacities progress through a series of stages or transformation; data seem to indicate that none of the stages can be skipped.

2. Some persons develop faster and further through the stages than others do. (About 60 percent of adults in our society are able to perform formal operations, whereas probably only 5–20 percent of all adults in our society are able to reason at the most complex level.)

3. Stages are defined by the reasoning process, not by issues, conclusions, emotion, behavior, or other kinds of motivations. This important distinction between the structure and the content of thought is the fundamental safeguard from misuse of structural developmental theory.

4. Persons seem to prefer the highest stage they can understand, but they usually cannot comprehend more than one stage above their own predominant stage.

5. Development in reasoning is a long-term process, and it is not automatic. It is stimulated by experience of cognitive conflict, exchange of varying views, and exposure to the next stage.

6. Persons appear to do most of their reasoning at one stage or at two adjacent stages.

7. Data suggest that the same stages are seen in all types of cultures, although the rate of development may vary, depending on stimulation from the culture. There seem to be no differences in the sequence of development through stages among Catholics, Protestants, Jews, Buddhists, Muslims, and atheists.[5]

8. Stages describe reasoning processes and *are not labels* to be attached to persons.

---

4. According to research reported by Renate Nummela Caine and Geoffrey Caine, the tremendous plasticity of the human brain demonstrates "that the physical structure of the brain changes as the result of experience." *Making Connections: Teaching and the Human Brain* (New York: Addison-Wesley, 1994), 30.

5. This claim is debated by a number of persons in Jeff Astley and Leslie J. Francis, eds., *Christian Perspectives on Faith Development: A Reader* (Grand Rapids, Mich.: Eerdmans, 1992).

9. Accurate determination of stages of reasoning is a complex process performed by trained scorers who check one another's conclusions. Any other procedure must be considered impressionistic *at best* and when properly checked is usually found to be inaccurate or invalid.

Perspectives of Faith as a Typology

Because structural development theory describes the transitions from simpler to more complex forms of cognition, many people naturally interpret the theory as a hierarchy from less advanced to more advanced stages of thinking. Such hierarchies can be detrimental when they are used to devalue and diminish persons representing the "lower" stages.[6] In years of teaching structural development theory in theological schools and churches, we have very often experienced persons interpreting the schema as such a hierarchy and either labeling themselves and others or thinking that it is their vocation to "move people along" to the "highest" (i.e., most complex) level. Some persons claim to have "developed" in their thinking simply by being exposed to one or all of the theories, and others use the stage descriptions to confirm the "inferiority" of persons who disagree with them!

To alleviate this problem, we experimented with various methods of presentation and discovered that the theory can be introduced and received more beneficially as a *typology* of perspectives. Describing the different perspectives as a typology of preferences in "ways that people think or approach matters" presents individuals with options for how they might view certain concepts or issues. The typology of perspectives forms an array that offers choices and challenges persons to articulate their preferences and to compare them with others'. Such an approach permits persons to explore more freely and comfortably the perspective or perspectives that inform their present way of making ethical decisions or understanding their day-to-day experiences.

Because our own research data were drawn from young adult and adult theological students, we described perspectives that correspond with conventional and postconventional categories of logical, moral, and faith development (i.e., the categories most commonly represented in adult populations). The intent was not to conceal the perspectives' grounding in developmental theories. In fact, we had students read the theories of Piaget, Kohlberg, Perry, and Fowler. Instead, we attempted to present persons with options to choose rather than a ladder to scale.[7] Table 1 shows how the

---

6. Rigid hierarchies tend to confine one's interpretations of difference to either inferiority or superiority. For an example of the argument that hierarchies inhibit creativity and cooperation, see Linda Jean Shepherd, *Lifting the Veil: The Feminine Face of Science* (Boston: Shambhala, 1993).

7. A similar attempt to tone down the hierarchical flavor of a developmental theory can be found in Belenky et al., *Women's Ways of Knowing*. The types of knowledge the authors

perspectives that we have identified appear to correlate with other theorists' categories.

Table 1
Correlations between Adult Faith Perspectives
and Other Theorists' Categories

Perspectives	Piaget	Kohlberg	Perry	Fowler	Parks	Belenky et al.
A	Low formal	Stage 3	Positions 1–3	Stage 3	Adolescent	Received knowledge
B		Stage 3½	Positions 4–6		Young adult	Subjective knowledge
C	High formal	Stage 4	Positions 7–9	Stage 4	Adult	Procedural knowledge
D		Stage 5		Stage 5	Mature adult	Constructed knowledge

In the course of our teaching, research, and application of these theories, the following typological profiles were developed to represent the perspectives of faith. Each one is a composite that attempts to convey an ideal type of that perspective; each is personalized with a fictional name reflecting a distinguishing characteristic. Categories or subject areas that were evaluated to determine the structure of each perspective are italicized.[8] These profiles should not be used as reductionist labels, but they may help persons keep in mind and respect the unique features and intrinsic value of each perspective of faith.

Perspective A: Affiliating Al

Affiliating Al views the *world* being centered on interpersonal relationships and as conforming to the values held by his significant others. His *reasoning* style is abstract and he is capable of formulating hypotheses, but he tends to compartmentalize and to merge thinking with feeling. For Al, *symbols* refer to abstract and personal realities that are bound together and cannot be changed without changing the realities themselves. Al has a strong emotional bond to the symbol and its "true meaning." His understanding of

---

describe closely resemble our four adult perspectives. However, in the authors' descriptions of received, subjective, procedural, and constructed knowledge, the first three kinds are still criticized, and the last is clearly favored as the appropriate goal toward which women should strive.

8. The profiles and table 2 on pages 22–23 were designed by drawing upon Piaget (see Inhelder and Piaget, *Growth of Logical Thinking*) and Fowler (*Stages of Faith*) for "Reasoning" and "Symbol," Wilcox (*Developmental Journey*) for "Social Perspective," Kohlberg (*Essays on Moral Development*) for "Justice," and Perry (*Forms of Intellectual and Ethical Development*) for "Self-understanding."

that bond is tacit in that he feels the symbol is important but cannot fully explain why. In this respect, he is not analytical.

In Al's social perspective, *persons* are stereotyped according to determining characteristics, for example, race, age, profession, or religion. Persons who are not part of his affiliate groups and do not conform to his values are considered odd, objectionable, or unworthy. Those who conform to his values are considered normal and acceptable. The *value of human life* is based on being loved and being good according to the values of Al's group. The degree to which a person loves or is loved would be a basis for determining that person's value. *Community/society* is demarcated in terms of affectional groups. Aggregates of such groups exclude people who are different. *Law* is interpreted as guidelines to define good behavior, to prevent chaos, and to create a better world. *Authority* is located in Al's affiliate group or in persons with admirable personal qualities that are sanctioned by his group; as such, authority is external and absolute. Al's *role-taking* ability is based on projecting himself into the feelings and ideas of others. This is limited by an inability to put himself in the place of another whose values, feelings, and thinking are substantially different from his own. For example, Al will have sympathy for the unfortunate if he feels it is deserved.

For Al, *justice,* or what is right, is interpreted in terms of conformity to conventional images of virtuous behavior. Good intentions, "correct" feelings, and doing good are some of the virtues that indicate what is right. Concern for intentions and affectional interpersonal relationships characterize Al's *self-understanding,* but he does not view himself as an agent to change others or the world.

Overall, Affiliating Al views life with a positive concern for feelings, mystery, and interpersonal relationships, whereas he has difficulty comprehending rationality and the function of systems and institutions.[9]

Perspective B: Bargaining Betty

Bargaining Betty sees the *world* as diverse and multiplistic and is concerned to express her own preferences. Her "bargain" is that others can have different preferences as long as they do not impose theirs on her. In return, she will not impose her preferences on others. This expectation of mutual respect and freedom reflects Betty's awareness that there are differing viewpoints and her uncertainty as to how one might evaluate their relative validity. Betty views the world through a variety of interpersonal relationships. Betty's *reasoning* style is abstract, so she is capable of formulating hypotheses and is interested in applying information in terms of its usefulness. Her reasoning tends to imitate analytical procedures by listing

---

9. In Perry's schema, this perspective represents "simple dualism," which is "a bifurcated structuring of the world between Good and Bad, Right and Wrong, We and Others" (*Forms of Intellectual and Ethical Development,* glossary; see also 59–71). Compare also with "received knowledge" as described in Belenky et al., *Women's Ways of Knowing.*

"reasons" to deal with issues of diversity, but she does not organize these into criteria in a logical process. *Symbols* are interpreted by Betty as abstract and personal realities with multiple meanings, and she has a strong emotional bond to the meanings she prefers. Although Betty's understanding of those feelings are tacit, she can grant the legitimacy of other persons' different feelings about the meaning of a symbol.

In Betty's social perspective, *persons* are categorized by certain stereotypes that she holds, but persons' differences are acknowledged and respected unless they threaten her own right to self-expression. The *value of human life* is based on her feelings about the importance of life in comparison to other values, such as money and the law. Betty views *community/ society* as consisting of multiple affectional groups, and she aligns herself with those groups that share her values and beliefs. Other groups are tolerated as long as they do not try to coerce others. *Law* is interpreted as the protection of one's right to live and to "do his or her own thing." Betty considers *authority* to be external and absolute, but she can relate to an authority in any way that is meaningful or feels right; she is not bound by others' opinions. In her *role-taking* ability, she understands a nonabsolutist perspective and may express impatience with those whose stance is absolutist.

Betty interprets *justice,* or what is right, in terms of conventional images of virtuous behavior. She gives some latitude to persons who do not conform, if they have good intentions and do not impose their behavior on others who do not approve of them. In her *self-understanding* as a bargainer, Betty thinks she is capable of making internal changes as well as influencing external factors that result in change and response from others. Overall, Bargaining Betty has positive concern for how persons differ because of their feelings about an idea or issue, but she has difficulty in clarifying and evaluating those differences based on criteria and critical thinking.[10]

Perspective C: Conceptualizing Charles

Conceptualizing Charles views the *world* as centered on explicit rational systems, concepts, and ideologies. His *reasoning* style is analytical and reflective, featuring a search for rationality characterized by clarity, coherence, and consistency. He has the ability to separate thinking from feeling, but he is often passionate about the concepts he holds to be valid. He tends

---

10. Perry identifies this structure of thinking as "multiplicity" and defines it as "a plurality of 'answers,' points of view, or evaluations, with reference to similar topics or problems. This plurality is perceived as an aggregate of discretes without internal structure or external relation, in the sense, 'Anyone has a right to his own opinion,' with the implication that no judgments among opinions can be made" (*Forms of Intellectual and Ethical Development,* glossary; see also 72–94). Compare with "subjective knowledge" as described in Belenky et al., *Women's Ways of Knowing.*

to dichotomize and polarize in an either/or fashion. Charles analytically separates *symbols* from the reality to which they refer. For him, a symbol can be "interpreted" (or demythologized) in terms of the concepts it "really" represents. He will make rational connections with the conceptual reality to which the symbol points.

In Charles's social perspective, *persons* are viewed in terms of their contribution to and maintenance of institutions or society. Hence, persons who do not share the beliefs and values of a system are excluded. Charles bases the *value of human life* on the priorities within a system and on one's contribution to the system. Responsibility, respect, and integrity are important virtues. Maintaining the social system and its legal rights has high priority. So, for example, although Charles may recognize the sacred value of animal life, he will probably attribute more value to human life, because humans are capable of thinking, choosing, caring, and contributing to society. Charles views *community/society* as structured by laws, rules, and sanctions that maintain the society. He excludes as invalid or unacceptable communities that are not bound by these structures. For Charles, *law* provides structures for the maintenance of society, institutions, and their values. Laws both value and protect persons' legal rights. Charles locates *authority* in systems and their credentialed representatives, but also within himself through his rational ability to determine valid concepts. His *role-taking* ability includes the recognition that each person lives in the context of a social system and may have a different experience or point of view based on that system and its contingencies. However, it may be difficult for Charles to understand and accept the framework of a different system.

Justice, or what is right, is understood by Charles in terms of the maintenance of "our" systems (institutions and society) and their values. He stresses persons' responsibility and contributions to those systems, as well as their legal rights. In Charles's *self-understanding*, he considers himself an agent of change, capable of affecting the world and conscious of his internal factors of change. Overall, Conceptualizing Charles articulates a positive concern for rationality, conceptual clarity, and understanding of the structure and function of institutions, but he often rejects feelings and mystery as sentimental or irrational.[11]

---

11. This perspective correlates with Perry's definitions of relativism and commitment. Relativism is "a plurality of points of view, interpretations, frames of reference, value systems and contingencies in which the structural properties of contexts and forms allow for various sorts of analysis, comparison and evaluation in Multiplicity" (*Forms of Intellectual and Ethical Development*, glossary; see also 95–133). Commitment is "an affirmation of personal values or choice in Relativism. A conscious act or realization of identity and responsibility. A process of orientation of self in a relative world. The word Commitment (capital C) is reserved for this integrative, affirmative function, as distinct from 1) commitment to an unquestioned or unexamined belief, plan or value, or 2) commitment to negativistic alienation or dissociation" (glossary; see also 134–76). Compare with "procedural knowledge" as described in Belenky et al., *Women's Ways of Knowing*.

Perspective D: Dialectical Donna

Dialectical Donna views the *world* in all of its ambiguous and paradoxical complexity. Yet she looks upon this pluralistic world with an integrating vision. Her *reasoning* style is abstract, analytical, dialectical, and paradoxical, moving toward creative integration. She has a critical self-awareness that allows her both to participate in systems (e.g., social, philosophical, religious) and to stand outside and reflect on them. Donna interprets *symbols* as both pointing to and participating in the reality they symbolize. She forms a relationship with the symbol in which feelings and ideas are integrated into a new vision. She thus embraces an emotional, rational, and aesthetic bonding with the symbol. Donna attests to the partiality and relativity of symbols while at the same time being grasped by the lure of symbols to see reality with new and more encompassing sight.

In Donna's social perspective, *persons* are viewed as individuals with dignity and intrinsic worth, as ends in themselves rather than as means to other ends. Hence, the *value of human life* is independent of limiting criteria, being rooted in the human ability to make moral decisions and to attribute meaning to the universe. Donna views *community/society* as open and inclusive, with boundaries that are created through social contract and due process. The latter are formalized in *laws* that preserve basic human rights, which underlie and can supersede societal and legal rights. Donna internalizes *authority* through her ability to weigh traditional authorities in a dialectical process. Her *role-taking* ability enables her to take the perspective of other persons to understand their social systems and worldviews in all of their complexity.

Donna perceives *justice,* or what is right, in terms of universal principles that undergird, inform, and transcend systems. For her, justice means the equality of basic rights and consideration that all persons are equal and of intrinsic worth. She determines what is just by balancing multiple moral and legal points of view. Donna holds an egalitarian *self-understanding* of herself and others as units of change capable of dialogue and mutual respect for all persons. Overall, Dialectical Donna integrates feelings, mystery, rationality, and systemic understanding, but she may have difficulty communicating with others who are not concerned with that kind of dialectical balance or who look for less complex solutions to life's problems.[12]

Perspectives of Faith as Structures of Thinking

As modes of cognition, perspectives of faith do not necessarily indicate *what* persons will conclude about a given issue or topic. They do indicate *how* persons will view, understand, and reason about that issue. The

---

12. Compare with "constructed knowledge" as described in Belenky et al., *Women's Ways of Knowing.* In our opinion, Perry's research does not yield data comparable to perspective D.

important distinction represents the difference between structures and contents of thought. Perspectives are *structures* of thinking that organize and
process *contents,* such as symbols of faith, doctrines or beliefs, authority,
relationships, and biblical texts.[13] Two persons interpreting the same ethical dilemma from the same perspective of faith might disagree completely
with one another. For example, Conceptualizing Charles's response to the
question "Should a person steal an expensive drug that will save his wife's
life?" could be either yes or no: yes, "because the commandment to save a
human life is actually the highest expression of law; no, "because although
some laws may not be completely fair or are unfair in some cases, in general
laws are made for and serve the common good and maintain the stability
of society."[14]

Each perspective of faith also has contrasting characteristics within its
own structure:

- *Perspective A:* A concern for feelings, for mystery, for interpersonal
  relationships. A lack of interest in rationality and in the function of
  institutions

- *Perspective B:* A concern for how persons differ because of the
  way they feel about an issue or idea. Difficulty in evaluating those
  differences based on criteria and critical thinking

- *Perspective C:* A concern for rationality and an ability to understand
  systems or institutions. Less interest in feelings and interpersonal relationships; often a rejection of mystery, of that which cannot be
  explained rationally

- *Perspective D:* A balanced concern for feelings, mystery, rationality,
  institutions. Difficulty in communicating with others who are not concerned with balance and who look for less complex solutions and
  answers

As structures of thinking, faith perspectives are necessarily cloaked in
content[15] and must be accessed through a style of questioning that gets

---

13. For a more comprehensive discussion about the distinction between structure and
content, see Parks, *Critical Years,* 101–6.

14. These examples are taken from pp. 6 and 78, respectively, of Lawrence Kohlberg et
al., *Standard Form Scoring Manual,* pt. 3, *Form A Reference Manual* (Cambridge: Center for
Moral Education, Harvard University, 1978), a manual prepared to score responses to moral
dilemmas. Kohlberg's "Heinz Dilemma," which we also used in our research, can be found
in appendix B. Similar examples of pro and con responses can be presented for the other
perspectives.

15. Similarly, our descriptions of the perspectives in this and following chapters must also
use content to express structure. For this reason, typologies for each perspective are not intended to be precise definitions. Rather, descriptions and illustrations should be treated more
as impressions that build on one another gradually to fill out an increasingly comprehensive
picture of a given perspective.

beneath the subject matter of an interview. Distinguishing between structure and content is a highly developed skill that is learned through training and experience in interviewing and in evaluating interviews. The interviewing method is designed to expose the structures of thought underlying the surface content, and results must be checked and rechecked by "blind" scoring processes. When people casually label others as representing a certain perspective, they often confuse content with structure. Therefore, we discourage hasty labeling that fixes typological stereotypes upon persons. The multitude of responses potentially expressed by each perspective demonstrates the perspectives' subtlety and complexity. Awareness of this complexity helps us understand a major source of misunderstanding and misinterpretation among adults in classes, on committees, at work, in the church, in politics, and in other communities and social structures.

Perspectives of Faith and Christian Nurture

Perspectives of faith provide a cognitive frame of reference for exploring the characteristics of adult faith and the diversity that accompanies its expressions. But what of growing in faith, as Paul exhorts in Ephesians: "Speaking the truth in love, we must grow up in every way into him who is the head, into Christ" (4:15 NRSV)? How does the church encourage growing or increasing knowledge of God in a way that communicates God's love and affirmation of the intrinsic value of all persons as they are?

Our approach to Christian education is consonant with Horace Bushnell's pioneering emphasis on nurture, or cultivation of a process that unfolds within an individual and in one's relationships with God and with others.[16] Nurturing the dynamic process of faith is not achieved by imposing information or discipline from without. It is not marked by comparisons or competition. It involves action and activities that foster inner transformation while attending to the unique qualities or gifts and needs of individuals, whether these are attributable to age, temperament, perspective, or something else.[17] It respects persons' present dispositions toward life and their ways of being in the world. Such nurture takes place through expanding, deepening, and enriching faith's perspectives on the various contents of religious life.

The goals or projected outcomes of this nurturing process are different for each religious group. That is, religious groups establish their own norms, images of maturity, and modal levels of the activity of faith.[18] The

---

16. Horace Bushnell, *Christian Nurture* (1861; reprint, Grand Rapids, Mich.: Baker, 1979, 1984), 30, 58. See also H. Edward Everding Jr., Clarence H. Snelling Jr., and Mary M. Wilcox, "A Shaping Vision of Community for Teaching in an Individualistic World: Ephesians 4:1–16 and Developmental Interpretation," *Religious Education*. 83, no. 3 (summer 1988): 423–37.

17. Bushnell, *Christian Nurture*, 51.

18. Craig Dykstra, "Faith Development and Religious Education," in *Faith Development*

goals may be portrayed biblically, psychologically, educationally, theologically, and so on. Nevertheless, we believe that the process of nurturing
Christian faith emphasizes at least these three main criteria:

1. *Integrity:* respecting and honoring the integrity of each person's faith
   activity and way of composing meaning through that activity

2. *Adequacy:* considering the adequacy of each person's faith activity for
   living in and coping with the individual's social and cultural context

3. *Opportunity:* providing each person the opportunity to increase in
   understanding and experience of God and the life of faith

The remaining chapters use these three criteria to illustrate how perspectives of faith can facilitate understanding and growth in a variety of life
contexts and through a number of processes for interacting with the contents of religious life. In summary, table 2 compiles the characteristics of
the four perspectives of adult faith outlined in this chapter.

---

and Fowler, ed. Craig Dykstra and Sharon Parks (Birmingham, Ala.: Religious Education
Press, 1986), 251–71.

Table 2
Adult Perspectives of Faith

Subject Area	Perspective A	Perspective B	Perspective C	Perspective D
World	Centered on interpersonal relationships, stereotypes; conforms to values of significant others	Multiplistic; centered on interpersonal relationships, one's preferences for diversity	An explicit rational system; centered on rationality, concepts, ideologies	A pluralistic, ambiguous, or complex unity; centered on vision, integration, basic rights. Can stand outside a system
Reasoning	Abstract, hypothetical, compartmentalized, not analytical, not clearly separated from feelings	Abstract, hypothetical; imitates analytical process, not clearly separated from feelings. Aware of diversity	Abstract, analytical, reflective, dichotomized. Searches for rationality, consistency, coherence; knows intellectual passion and wonder.	Abstract, dialectical, paradoxical; moving toward integration. Has critical self-awareness
Symbol (Person, object, story, thing, etc.)	Refers to an abstract and personal reality to which it is bound; cannot be changed without changing the reality. Emotive bonding with symbol	Has multiple meanings; refers to an abstract reality to which it is bound. A bonding with the symbol and its reality through one's feelings and preferences	Rationally separated from the conceptual reality to which it refers. Rational but passionate bonding to the conceptual reality	Joined with the reality and one's feelings and ideas into a new vision. Emotional-rational-aesthetic bonding
Social perspective: Persons	Capable of stable and continuing affectional relationships, but stereotyped by limiting characteristics determined by one's affiliate group	Have different limiting characteristics, but acknowledged and valued as long as they do not impose their differences on others	Instrumental to society if they share concepts and values of a system; excluded if they do not share society's values	Ends rather than means to ends; each has ultimate worth and dignity, equality
Value of human life	Based on being loved and good according to values of one's group	Based on feelings about the importance of life in comparison with other values	Based on values of a system and one's contribution to the system	Based on intrinsic value of each life, independent of limiting criteria
Community/ society	Affectional groups that exclude people who are different	Multiple affectional groups. Aligns with group according to preferences; tolerates others if they are not coercive	Structured by laws, rules, sanctions that maintain the society and its values; exclusive	Open, inclusive; created through social contract, due process

Table 2 (continued)
Adult Perspectives of Faith

Subject Area	Perspective A	Perspective B	Perspective C	Perspective D
Law	Guidelines for good behavior to prevent chaos, create a better world	Protection for persons' chosen preferences	Protection of legal rights, social stability; structures and maintains society, institutions, and their values	Preservation of basic human rights, which are prior to law; formalization and result of social contracts
Authority	Located in one's group or in persons with admirable qualities sanctioned by one's group; external	Located in one's preferences, which shape how one relates to external and absolute authority	Located in the system and its credentialed representatives, in logically determined truth; also internalized within the individual	Located in the weighing of traditional authorities in a dialectical process; internalized
Role-taking	Based on projection into feelings of others if not too different from oneself; empathy for the "unfortunate," if deserved	Based on tolerance for letting people "do their own thing" as long as they do not impose on others. Understands nonabsolutist perspective, engages in some stereotyping	Based on taking the role of others in context of similar social systems and values	Based on taking the role of persons, groups, other worldviews. Can step outside individual's and system's points of view
Justice (what is right)	Good intentions, right feelings, conformity to conventional images of good behavior	Conformity to conventional images of good behavior; tolerance for people who do not conform, if they have good intentions and do not impose behavior on others	Maintenance of "our" systems and their values, responsibility to the system (church, society), contributions to society	Universal principles, equality of basic rights, equal worth of all persons; a balance of moral and legal points of view
Self-understanding	World affects individual; individual not agent of change on others or the world. Capable of internal change	World affects individual; individual not agent of change on others or the world; live and let live. Capable of internal change	Self is agent of change, capable of affecting world. Conscious of internal change	Egalitarian; all persons capable of dialogue and effecting change; mutual respect for persons as ends and not means

2

Perspective A:
AFFILIATING AL

[The scriptures] have authority because God said they have authority!
— Al$_2$[1]

Al's Interpreting Style

When Al interprets 2 Timothy 3:14–17 (see page 7), he tends to focus on abstract meanings or guidelines that are personal, true, and authoritative. Al$_1$ (male, age 21) focuses on the abstract and generalized meaning of "usefulness." *What do you feel stands out for you in this biblical text?* "That the scriptures are useful." *Why is that particularly significant to you?* "That they are useful, well, because I am studying to be a minister and I should hope that they are useful in some way."

Al$_2$ (female, age 43) applies the text in an abstract but uncritical way, indicating an understanding of authority as external and absolute ("God's plan"). *What do you think is the main point of the text?* "For me the main point is not that the Bible has been divinely inspired or some such thing. You can also take the knowledge that you are going to get, because that is where we are in seminary, and do something with it because that also is God's plan for us."

Al$_3$ (female, age 37) abstracts meaning on the level of personal inspiration and support. His response also seems to understand scripture as an external authority. *What stands out for you in this biblical text?* "I think the text is an inspiration to teachers of the scripture, Bible scripture, to teach others, and also a support of teachers in trying times, that they might have to reflect back on scripture for their own support."

---

1. Al is a fictitious character composed of quotations from various subjects in our research who represent perspective A. Subscripts denote these different individuals. We use the same method to describe perspectives B, C, and D.

24

Al's View of the Authority of the Bible

Al perceives the authority of the Bible as existing independently of his interpretation of it. It provides normative guidelines or doctrines that are sanctioned by the group with which he is affiliated. Its authority may be described in terms of inerrancy, a canon within the canon, *sola scriptura*, or other standard. Al's form of reasoning about authority is often tacit and stereotypical.

Al_1 responds as follows to *What reasons would you give to someone for the authority of scripture?* "I guess I would say that the authority I give to the scripture is basically presenting the values, accepting the values presented in the scriptures, and I don't know if I can give any reason why for one value being better than another. Values are based on...so it is kind of a faith of accepting the authority." *And opposed to that, you would not necessarily accept the values of Socrates or Plato or Kant or Tillich or whoever?* "I would accept their values insofar as they illumined the values presented in the Bible." Authority is understood tacitly as an external standard with generalized and abstract meaning (i.e., "values").

Al_2 perceives the Bible's authority as absolute and external in response to *What reasons would you give to someone for the authority of the scriptures?* "Yes, they have authority because God said they have authority!"

Al's View of Tradition

Al understands tradition in connection with his affectional grouping of people with whom he finds meaning. Tradition can also suggest to him a historical entity that generally is past but can be passed on.

Al_2 views tradition interpersonally when responding to *What functions as tradition for you?* "My upbringing, my mother, my father, my pastors, my church, my relationship with others, my learning."

Al_3 views tradition as both an aggregate of personal experience and an abstract and objective historical entity. *What functions as tradition for you?* "There are two kinds of tradition: personal heritage and that [which] has come down through the ages....It would have to encompass both of these things, my own personal tradition, my life, my family, my background, and also it would have to look at the tradition of mankind's tradition, coming down through the ages."

Al_4 (male, age 24) views tradition as external to himself and the present. He can then "add a few things to it, and pass it on"

> The tradition is the passing down of what others have acquired. As the human race goes on and on, there is more...tradition to be passed down....I see myself as being at the end of tradition. The

tradition is past. Maybe I have a different idea of tradition. I see tradition as history, and there are a lot of traditions that I come through: my family, Christianity, which denomination of Christianity. There [are] a lot of traditions that make up what my tradition is. I see myself as tradition leads up to me, and then from me tradition is carried on, so there is going to be some proof and reproof of the tradition. I am going to take the tradition that was handed down to me from my parents, filter some things, add a few things to it, and pass it on.

Al's Images of the Bible

Images of the Bible for Al are characteristically multidimensional, uncritically apprehended, and focused on one type of meaning, such as providing examples, guidelines, and instructions. Al_1 shares images that are replete with feelings and interpersonal relationships. *When you think of the Bible, what pictures, words, or phrases come to mind?* "I suppose a lot.... Jesus sitting down and all the little kids gathered around, the verse in Matthew about clothing the naked, and visiting those in prison, and feeding the hungry, and doing to the least of these my brethren, you did it unto me." In response to the next questions, Al_1 rejects a literalist image but does consider what can be useful in the message or implied values of the Bible. *What are your feelings or thoughts about the Bible?* "I think it contains useful things, especially in the area of values, what you ought to do, but I don't think it is a science textbook. I don't think it is infallible. I think that the writers probably made mistakes, and it shouldn't be worshiped." *What role does the Bible play in your life?* "Provides me with values to live by. That is the main role...the life of Jesus Christ, a working model, and how values can be realized."

Al_2 presents a stereotypical picture of Jesus characterized by an interpersonal and affectional pattern of thinking. *When you think of the Bible, what pictures, words, or phrases come to mind?* "I am very oriented to just the concept of what Jesus was in my mind, of what I have picked up, which is his being very human, caring, shepherd-type person that nurtured and loved us, people, and from that all those positive things, doing for and unto others." In the following statement, Al_2 focuses on the message and the penumbra of mystery associated with his image of the Bible. *What are your feelings or thoughts about the Bible?* "My feelings or thoughts are positive.... There is an element of mystery of the Bible. I have an aura of excitement about [it] at this point in my life, being able to explore that book which has always been so elusive to me, and this time I can ask its meaning and to be able to interpret it to a degree."

Al_3 seems to struggle with new information, but he still thinks of the Bible's message in terms of objective and unquestioned meaning. *When you think of the Bible, what pictures, words, phrases come to mind?* "Well, I think the most predominant thing that comes to mind in studying the Old Testament is obeying the will of God, and he will be with you as you do that." *What are your feelings about the Bible?* "Well, first of all, a sacred document. Second of all, in contrast to that I would have to say I am sure it is fallible. It is also an historical document, but in the end I think the essence of it, what is said continuously throughout the Bible, reigns as the highest truth of mankind."

In response to the questions about the role of the Bible, AI_4 focuses on its external authority to teach exemplary behavior. "I see the Bible as an instructor...that says you are an example to the people....The scripture says you are an example to others and if they see it as being wrong to use that same type of thing (for example, drinking alcohol), then you should be able to conform to their wishes so that they would not [stumble]."

AI's Understanding of Truth

For AI, truth is absolute and abstract. It is right or wrong. It is based on the quantity of knowledge that experts have attained, experts who function as external authorities.

AI_2 displays an understanding of a hidden absolute in his insistence on the limitations of his knowledge and in his disbelief about "anybody's theories." His personal and affectional image of Jesus is also consistent with this perspective. *Do you feel that your understanding of the Bible is true?* "My knowledge is so limited, I don't believe that what I believe about the Bible is false. I do believe that Jesus was a loving, caring man and [that] these scriptures were written about him. I guess what I think I know right now is true....I guess I don't feel that at any point I'm going to believe anybody's theories."

AI_5 (female, age 30) mentions his limited knowledge, acquired by a great deal of work, and God as the absolute authority (e.g., "what he wants you to know"). *Do you feel your understanding of the Bible is true?* "Yes. That is an open-ended yes. I haven't learned everything about the Bible. It is an ongoing thing. But, I guess, primarily I believe what I believe up to this point because of many agonizing hours spent in meditating on different points and situations. I have accepted that peace that comes when you feel that you have reached what he wants you to know."

AI_6 (male, age 24) understands truth in terms of right and wrong; hence, he expects an absolute or correct understanding. Moreover, the true understanding is based on the quantity of knowledge attained by people who study the Bible more (i.e., the implied experts). *Do you feel that your understanding of the Bible is true?* "Not necessarily. Because I am not infallible. I don't think I have a broad enough knowledge of the Bible to know whether I am right or wrong in my feelings." *Are understandings of the Bible other than your own true?* "Yes. I think there are a lot of people who know more about the Bible, who understand the Bible better than I do, and their feelings about the Bible are more true." *How do you know that their feelings are more true than yours?* "Well, they have studied it and they understand it better. I think they can grasp easier what the Bible is talking about, more so than what I am still struggling with and haven't spent enough time with it to completely understand it."

Al$_7$ (female, age 41) acknowledges that his understanding is incomplete but that further knowledge will not alter his "concept of the Bible as inspired" or his "view of God or Christ." These are, for him, "universal" concepts. That is, they represent for him an absolute view of truth. *Do you feel that your understanding of the Bible is true?*

> I feel that my understanding of the Bible is incomplete. I feel that I can believe what I understand so far. I believe that is true. But I also believe that I have not studied [enough] and that in studying these parts I will get a little broader view of God and his son and the work that they've done on this earth. But I would say now that I do not think this increased learning...will change my concept of the Bible as inspired or change my view of God or Christ.

Al's Way of Thinking of Self as Interpreter

Al's understanding of himself as an interpreter is characterized by a sense of growth or internal change that is often expressed in a rejection of literalist thinking and an acceptance of abstract formulations. While living within a dualistic true/false world, Al may at times experience confusion about the diversity of people's truth claims.

Al$_1$ rejects literal understandings but has a stereotypical understanding and valuing of usefulness. His doubts about the facticity of miracles and the Book of Revelation reveal his focus on the personal, on sympathy, and on one's good intentions: *Are there areas in which you wonder or have deep doubts about the Bible?* "That [miracles] are actually supernatural events, that God put his finger down and changed the natural course of events....Well, because [the Book of Revelation] is very bloody and warlike, and you don't know how useful [it could be]." He is aware of his capacity to change but is vague in his understanding of how that comes about. *Do you feel that you are changing, growing, struggling in your understanding of the Bible?* "Oh, I have always been going though process of change. It is hard for me to say where I am heading right now and in the future, but you know, when I look back in the past, I see certain progress or growth, so I assume that I am changing now because I always have in the past."

Al$_2$ comments that the experience of being interviewed causes him to see clearly the areas where the truth is unambiguous for him. *Anything else to add to this interview?* "Only that for myself the first interview shows me clearly my conflict on what I believe to be my personality which is lots of shades of gray and lots of shades of gray for my value system, and a clear-cut identification of where I am with my blacks and whites, which are also very clear-cut, but I don't identify them as easily." His "shades of gray" suggest that there are other areas where he feels confused, like he is sitting in the middle of a whirlwind. Such experiences of conflict are early indicators of a potential shift to another perspective that may more adequately account for or "fit" one's experience.

Al₃ seems to be on the verge of developing another perspective because of signs of change he is beginning to notice. *Do you feel you are changing, growing, struggling in your understanding of the Bible?* "Yes, I do. I wasn't nearly familiar enough with the Bible before I came to seminary. I hope that will be the concentration of my studies while I am here. I am beginning to see, just beginning to see the seeds of change from what I studied."

Al₄ questions a literal understanding of the Bible and yet is hesitant to accept his own abstracted understandings. *Are there areas in which you wonder or have deep doubts about the Bible?* "I wonder about all the miracles of the Bible. A lot of the time I interpret the raising of Lazarus...I have trouble with that. It is not that I don't believe in it. It is that I wonder if maybe something else wasn't meant by it." Perfect knowledge is no longer attainable for this interpreter. *Do you feel that you are changing, growing, struggling in your understanding of the Bible?* "There is going to be a lot of struggle. I don't think that I am going to know everything about the Bible...[and] what is meant for me being here in seminary. The day comes that I should die and go to my eternal glory, or my eternal damnation, whichever, I'm still not going to know everything, because of the matter of interpretation."

Al₈ (male, age 22) anticipates the need for a new structure of thinking. *Do you feel that you are changing, growing, struggling in your understanding of the Bible?* "Oh, yeah, definitely — especially coming to seminary. It's really opening my eyes. I'm starting to think about things I never thought about....I'm going to have to have some type of form, not a set form, but a format I'm going to have to follow."

Summary and Table

Al's faith perspective sees a right or wrong world, a true or false world. The group with which he identifies sets the norms for determining the absolute truths of the Bible and the correct past traditions that he can pass on to others. The content that takes center stage for Al's normative group could be literary-critical biblical scholarship, pietistic evangelicalism, feminist theology, or any number of other subject areas. The illustrations from our research data reflect the influences of the learning environment of a "liberal" graduate school of theology that values new information and critical thinking. That is, these students were expected to change and, for the most part, they adapted to that expectation. For example, Al_2 has become very aware of "my blacks and whites," and Al_6 knows that "I'm going to have to have some type of form" with which to think differently.

Although the structure of our thinking forms the essential framework for meaning, content also plays a significant role in enhancing (or restricting) the broadening, enriching faith potential for each perspective. Content includes not only ideas, images, and concerns, but also the covert and implicit expectations and norms of the environment in which one's thinking takes place. Whatever the content, Al identifies truths as those personal guidelines, examples, and doctrines which provide an abstract but clear set of directions for what he can interpret from the Bible and apply to his life. Some Als may see themselves grounded in absolute truths that they uncritically and tacitly apprehend, whereas other Als see themselves as alive to a world of abstract ideas that enable them to soar beyond a concrete and literal world of biblical interpretation. Table 3 organizes and summarizes the distinctive features of Al's perspective of faith on biblical interpretation.

Table 3
Al's Faith Perspective on Biblical Interpretation

Subject Area	Al's Faith Perspective
World	Centered on interpersonal relationships, stereotypes; conforms to values of significant others
Reasoning	Abstract, hypothetical, compartmentalized, not analytical, not clearly separated from feelings
Symbol	Refers to an abstract and personal reality to which it is bound; cannot be changed without changing the reality. Emotive bonding with symbol
Authority	Located in one's group or in persons with admirable qualities sanctioned by one's group; external
Self-understanding	World affects individual; individual not agent of change on others or the world. Capable of internal change
Interpreting style	Focuses on the abstract and on true meanings, guidelines, and what is useful
Authority of the Bible	External and absolute; tacit and stereotypical
Tradition	An affectional aggregation; a past historical entity
Images of the Bible	Multidimensional, uncritically apprehended; having one meaning, such as guidelines and examples
Truth	Absolute, abstract, right or wrong
Self as interpreter	Feels sense of growth and internal change; anticipates struggle with diversity

3

Perspective B:
BARGAINING BETTY

*I would affirm that the scripture is the word of God, but not always.
... And I would state very clearly that this is my opinion only and is
not absolute and is not the final word.* — Betty₃

Betty's Interpreting Style

When Betty interprets 2 Timothy 3:14–17 (see page 7), she tends to focus
on the message, guidelines, or instructions that she feels are useful and
workable, but she does not assume that these are necessarily applicable to
anyone else. Her way of thinking rejects explicit, absolute understandings
of the Bible, because she recognizes diversity within it or within interpretations of it, but she may still long for a hidden absolute as something
consistent that can be relied upon.

Betty₁ (male, age 21) holds an external view of authority ("the things
that have to be done") but bases the differences of interpretation she finds
upon "the way a person feels." *What do you think is the main point of
the text?* "If you take all these things, all these things will fit together and
you'll have the closeness to God that's desired by most everyone." *Are you
saying you agree or disagree with the text?*

> I agree with the things that have to be done, but I disagree with the
> fact that they have to be just that, I guess. I don't feel it takes into
> consideration the real feeling of the person, that sort of thing, and I
> think that's an important part of it, too, the way a person feels. He
> may have a legitimate reason why he feels that way; and why would
> I argue with him if he truly believes that way? Maybe he feels he's
> gotten close to God the way he is.

Betty₂ (male, age 29) interprets the text in terms of an abstract concept
or message ("foundation") that is applicable to one's experience and that
should be instructive. *What do you think is the main point of the text?*
"Basically, I would say that it wants you to know that what you have

learned in the past is very important.... You established a foundation to this point, and you should use that foundation throughout the rest of your life." *What do you feel about the text?* "I agree with it because I see that is what has happened in my life. It has been affirmed in my life." *Would you summarize what you think the text is all about?*

> The foundations are very important, and you should continue to build upon [them]. It also uses all the tools that you learned in that growing-up period to, again, add to your life. You shouldn't discount them even though some of them are bad and some of them are good. Basically, the point is that the Bible is something that is constantly in use, one of those tools. It is something that should be used.

Betty₃ (male, age 32) rejects the Bible as infallible or absolute. She is aware of its "contradictions" and inconsistencies. Yet she thinks it can still provide "unfailing" guidance, which for her is an implicit absolute. *What do you think is the main point of the text?* "I agree that what you have learned is very important in the Christian context.... Let it be your guide as you go on in becoming truly the man of God." *Do you agree or disagree?* "I agree with the portion that says don't abandon what you have learned. The inference there is that what you have learned is good, and one should never abandon what he has learned that is good. The disagreement is also the inference that the Bible is infallible, that the Bible cannot be questioned or refuted." *Why do you disagree?* "I am not a biblical scholar, but the formation of the Bible, for example, from all that was written in early Christian history was, at best, a haphazard process. The Bible offers many contradictions. My feeling is that if the Bible was divinely inspired, there would not be so much inconsistency in it." *Can you summarize what you think the scripture is all about?* "The text is encouragement. It is encouragement in saying that what you have been doing is good.... Keep at it, but also move forward, that you have more to learn. But never lose sight of the fact that the Bible is an unfailing guide to lead you into righteousness, that the Bible is an index of how one becomes right with God."

Betty's View of the Authority of the Bible

Betty understands the authority of the Bible in terms of her personal feelings or preferences. Like Al, she treats its authority as external and absolute, but Betty thinks persons can relate to it in any way that is meaningful for them or feels right to them.

Betty₂ accepts a diversity of understandings of the Bible's authority in response to the question *What reasons would you give someone for the authority of scripture?* "I have been in places where it has been absolutely impossible for me to get across my understanding of how the Bible is an authority for me. But the Bible is an authority for other people in a different understanding. If I can find out about their understandings and how that relates to them, then I can use that and show them how the Bible is their authority as well."

Betty$_3$ rejects literal thinking about authority and distinguishes her "opinion" from what is nonnegotiable. *What reasons would you give to someone for the authority of the scriptures?*

> I would affirm that the scripture is the word of God, but not always.... And I would state very clearly that this is my opinion only and is not absolute and is not the final word. But I would convey to a young man that he needs to study and understand what is in the Bible, that most of it does represent God's word, but also one must realize [that] because it was written by man, it is vulnerable to deviate from God's word.

Betty$_4$ (female, age 40) is clear about God's "ultimate authority," and although the Bible does not dictate the truth, it does provide core meanings that are trustworthy, "workable," and relatively unambiguous. *What reasons would you give to someone for the authority of scripture?*

> All scripture is inspired by God, I would say would be the main thing. The essence of the Bible comes through as something that human beings can cling to, that has good, workable knowledge and insights for us to go from. I guess I'll just have to say the authority comes from the inspiration of God to people who care about wanting to impart faith to others, and what they have gained from it.... God is the ultimate authority.

Betty$_5$ (female, age 41) is prepared to question the authority of the Bible as having absolute answers to "impose" on others, but she is not able to support this point of view with clear and logical reasons ("I am not sure"). *What reasons would you give to someone for the authority of scripture?*

> I'm not sure. I think my first reaction would really be to question the authority rather than to say to anyone, "This is what you must believe." It is really necessary to question before you can either accept it or reject it. I really feel very strongly that it is hard to impose that on people even though there is something right about it. There is something wrong about saying, "This is the answer for you and everybody else." I am not sure.

Betty's View of Tradition

Like Al, Betty understands tradition interpersonally, as a grouping of people with whom she finds meaning and/or externally and historically as something in the past that can be passed on. However, Bargaining Betty is aware that there are lots of different traditions and that there are those who question her own tradition(s). She may begin to look for a rational conception of tradition that helps her fit these differences into a more coherent picture.

Betty$_2$ understands tradition globally in terms of human needs or bonds with one another that can be bad or good. She is aware of differences in traditions but will not impose hers on other people. Tradition provides an order for her life that seems to consist of moral guidelines and proper intentions. *What functions as tradition for you?* "Tradition functions for me in the fact that human beings have an existence.... It's like our roots. If we don't have any existence, then the human being is cut off from other human beings. Tradition therefore comes through as our root structure for other human beings.... So, tradition becomes changeable and sometimes bad as well as good." *What kinds of traditions function in your life?* "Basically...education.... Church is a tradition.... Tradition functions as an order for my life. My parents taught me certain things that I still perceive in my life.... I see difference in other people, too, so I don't put that tradition on other people. I use the things they taught me.... You know, be nice, be courteous.... Those are traditions for me."

Betty$_4$ understands tradition in terms of her personal experiences with family and church, which provide "security" and a sense of God's presence. She is comfortable with "questioning" different interpretations, but she also affirms an "essence" of truth about God and faith. *What functions as tradition for you?* "The security of the church which I have had all my life in various denominations, the sense of the rightness for me.... I have a strong faith tradition through my father and mother and grandmother, and a sense, very much the sense of the presence of God working in those lives." *How do you understand yourself in relation to that tradition?*

> It just makes me feel more secure as I get older. I went through a period of not wanting to question anything, because I didn't want to have to upset all the things I believed, but then when I did start to question, I just found out it wasn't a question of the essence of God or faith itself. It was a questioning of some of the "man-words" of interpretations of things, and ultimately you have to have your own interpretation, and so my interpretations — which I know I will grow in — different insights...it just makes the tradition that much more deeply rooted.

Betty$_5$ considers tradition to be the "foundation" that people receive and build on in their own ways. However, tradition is not as "authoritative" as the Bible, which exists as something apart from the influence of people and time. For her, the Bible's objective "message" holds absolute truth "for all the ages." *What is the function of tradition for you?* "It really gives people an important basis, more understanding. Even though comprehension levels are different, there needs to be an effort of establishing tradition. It is just like building a foundation for someone. You need to have a point from which to take off, to build on, something to establish your quality of learning." *What is more important to you, the Bible or tradition?* "I guess the Bible would be more authoritative. The Bible would be more valid than tradition. It is my feeling that the Bible has a way, a message for all the ages. It is an all-encompassing kind of situation. Tradition is more tied to a certain age, more limited in connection with the times and experiences of other people."

Betty$_6$ (male, age 21) understands tradition as "guidelines" from the past experiences of others, but she places that understanding within the context of the multiplicity of traditions and other types of instruction. Nevertheless, Betty$_6$ is aware that her tradition is "directed" by God in something like a tacit reference to an authority that she considers unquestionable. *What functions as tradition for you?* "The traditions to me give me guidelines as to what has happened in the past and let me see how others' choices were handled and how I might handle them." *How do you understand yourself in relation to tradition?* "It is important because it is a way of learning, showing me, but it isn't the most vital, because there are many things that go into learning, and tradition is just one of them." *What is more important to you, Bible or tradition?* "The Bible, because the Bible is in a way...based on my tradition. There are many traditions in mankind that aren't God directed, God influenced."

Betty's Images of the Bible

Images of the Bible for Betty are typically multidimensional but uncritically apprehended. She thinks about the Bible's message or meaning in terms of its examples, guidelines, and instructions. However, she is also aware of different meanings and interpretations and that the apparent message may not have the same significance for everyone.

Betty$_1$ rejects literal anthropomorphic images for the Bible and expresses some confusion about how to decide what are appropriate interpretations. She concludes that there are several "different meaning[s]," making the Bible important but "not the ultimate" truth. *When you think of the Bible, what pictures, words, or phrases come to mind?*

> A man sitting there with a kind of ghost figure behind, with his hand on his shoulder saying, "Write this, this, and this," but that's the first thing that comes to my mind. But then it wasn't quite like that. These men, the people who did write it, they were human beings. They could have made mistakes, misinterpreted, things like that. I guess at this point I don't see [it] as blindly written, as I did when I was back in Sunday school. It's not a complete turnaround...and that causes

more problems...what do I believe and what don't I believe? What is valid and what isn't valid? And it was so much easier back then, but I don't see it like that.

What are your feelings or thoughts about the Bible? "It's important in directing our lives...but it doesn't mean that this is the only possible way to take into account the human aspects....[It's] not the ultimate, but it is important. I think 'ultimate' is the answer for everything...that God...[is] ultimate, nothing [is] greater. He encompasses all." *What role does the Bible play in your life?* "It takes on different meaning at different times. At the present time, it is a means for inspiration. At other times, if I'm using it as a teaching device, it is something else. It depends upon the time of what I am looking for it to be."

Betty₄ identifies the Bible with pleasant personal feelings and images. Even though she understands the Bible in an absolute sense as the word of God, she sees multiple meanings within it ("different qualities") that can give her assurance in a variety of ways and times. *When you think of the Bible, what pictures, words, or phrases come to mind?* "The gentleness, the warmth and the love and the quality of understanding, the openness on God's part, the quality of Jesus going against [what was] legal in those days, because people meant more to him....I find so many things that tie in with the way he did stuff that make me feel good about my relationship to humanity." *What role does the Bible play in your life?* "It is like I am thinking of the book that was personally written for me on occasion, and it makes me feel secure, like somebody answered a question of mine....So it plays a special role, because there are so many aspects that touch on so many aspects of my life. It isn't just a book but it is the word of God, period. It has so many different qualities for different moods."

Betty₅ admits that her understanding of the Bible is "confused" right now. She sees multiple images and meanings at the same time that she remains confident of its significance. At this point she cannot sort out analytically how both can be true. *What are your thoughts and feelings about the Bible?* "I sometimes have difficulty in accepting it on the basis of really being, uh, inspired by God. And yet, at the same time, it contains things that really do seem inspired and inspiring. I have conflict about which way is really right." *Why are these important for you?* "They are important as examples of how people have lived bringing something out of chaos, or bringing an improvement over situations that had been in the past. It helps you make the most out of whatever happens." *What role does the Bible play in your life?*

I remember [that] as a child the Bible was a very important part of our life. To my family it was a significant part. Right now, you know, I really feel confused in my understanding of it. I feel that there is something very important about [it], but I don't know how to describe that kind of significance — an intuitive feeling that there really is something valuable there, but how to make that specific, I don't understand.

Betty₇ (male, age 22) images the Bible as a guide that is "absolute" for herself but is "not absolute" for other people. *What are your feelings or thoughts about the Bible?* "It is a guideline in the way that I should live my life. I see it as, you know, it could have mistakes, but as far as the general guidelines . . . not absolute, but absolute for me, in a sense . . . because I cannot say what is absolute for somebody else, because I feel like that would be . . . interfering with that person's rights."

Betty's Understanding of Truth

For Betty, truth is whatever each person feels is true. Truth can be different for different people (until it interferes with "my" truth). The only criterion for deciding among competing truth claims is "what feels right." Nevertheless, truth is derived from external authority, in that there is absolute truth "out there" somewhere, but we cannot always discover what it is.

Betty₁ thinks of the Bible's truth in terms of what is "good" for her, but she understands and accepts diversity in terms of what other persons "feel" is meaningful in it. *Do you feel your understanding of the Bible is true?* "I'm limited in what I understand of it. It for me is good, but I can't expect it to be good for anyone else." *Are understandings of the Bible other than your own true?* "I'll never argue with a person about a point in the Bible, because I feel that that's what he feels, that's what he gets out of it, that's the meaning that he finds in it. . . . It may not be what I believe, but I'll take his point of view, because I'm not the judge. . . . It's not my job to tell someone that's wrong or that's right."

Betty₈ (female, age 21) expresses her understanding of multiplicity in terms of persons having their own opinions about what is true. There seems to be no basis to judge the truth or falsity of different opinions other than each individual's own ideas. *Do you feel that your understanding of the Bible is true?* "It is true for me, but I'm not going to say it is true for anyone else." *Why do you think that?* "Well, they have their opinion and I have mine. I am not going to say that mine is wrong and theirs is right and that mine is true and theirs is false, because they have found through some sort of reasoning process that this is true for them. It is not for me to judge what is true and false for other people. No one can do that."

Betty₉ (female, age 38) thinks about truth in terms of what has "worked" in her life. She accepts understandings and feelings of others if not too different from her own, and bases that acceptance on how others "feel about it." *Do you feel that your understanding of the Bible is true?* "For myself, yes, I feel that my understanding of the Bible is true, because it's worked for me. It's worked for me in understanding myself, and . . . it's worked because when I share some of my understandings with others or explore with others, I come to new understandings and different interpretations." *Do you feel that others' understandings that are different from your own are also true?*

> I choose to be with people who share more of an understanding that I share. . . . I sometimes have a problem with other people whose understandings are different, and I guess I have to go back to what I said earlier . . . who's wrong and who's right? And I have learned to accept that that's how they have to feel about it. But I sure like the chance to suggest another meaning to them, whether they are willing to accept it or not, just as they want to give me another meaning.

Betty's Way of Thinking of Self as Interpreter

Betty both questions absolutes and seeks a way to account for a multi-plistic world with its competing truth claims. Her feelings, intentions, and personal relationships are very important, but she is not a passive player in the world. She views herself as capable of affecting other people and various external factors in her life, and she is aware of how her decisions can impact her own internal changes.

Betty$_3$ struggles to "reconcile" the differences between what she feels is right and "what the Bible says." She begins to identify a process in which she checks the appropriateness of her interpretation by seeking concurrence with a variety of people. She is very sensitive to ways she has changed and anticipates that her faith will continue to change through life. *Are there areas in which you wonder or have deep doubts about the Bible?* "There have been many occasions where I have struggled to reconcile something that I feel is right with something that is written in the Bible . . . so the feeling is that something is wrong with me and nothing is wrong with the Bible." *What persons or communities have been most influential in shaping your understanding of the Bible?* "It is just something that has gradually evolved, and I am sure that it has a long, long ways to go. I feel that the understanding that I have is only the tip of the iceberg of what understanding I may eventually have." *Where has your understanding been drawn from?* "Personal intuition . . . [a course] in church history . . . and then checking whatever insights you think you've reached with . . . a variety of people . . . and viewing their response to what I have said about the Bible, and usually if that response is one of concurrence, then I feel like my understanding has some credibility." *Do you feel that you are changing, growing in your understanding of the Bible?* "I definitely feel that I am growing and I am struggling. . . . I am sure that three or four years from now, I will feel much differently than I do now about different aspects of my Christian life, or about life in general."

Betty$_4$ expresses lots of doubts about the Bible that have sprung from all the new information she has gained in school. Her faith in the Bible's essential truth remains firm, yet she is experiencing an internal change, "a whole new perspective." *Are there areas in which you wonder or have deep doubts about the Bible?* "There are. I have real questions about the essences of the parables.... I wonder about the Bible in the context of the civilization that was going on, the writing that was going on, all the changing qualities of civilization which would be able to have an effect on it.... Any doubts that I would have would be offset by the fact that I believe it to be the inspiration of God." *Do you feel that now you are changing and growing and struggling in your understanding of the Bible?*

> Oh, yes, I am more aware of that than ever ... probably because I am confronted with so much now, all that people have questioned.... I just realize that I am looking at it in a whole new perspective, for one thing. The spiritual perspective is already there, but the outlook of gaining some wisdom from it, too, in a more solid foundation of faith. It is very exciting to know that there is so much of my head in this.

Betty$_{10}$ (female, age 38) rejects blind acceptance of absolutes but seems to be groping for a reasonable way to deal with conflicts, decision making, and her self-understanding. *Are there areas in which you wonder or have deep doubts about the Bible?* "I guess so. I guess my doubt is that ... I question the idea that so many people blindly ... place so much emphasis on a thing or book." *Do you feel that you are changing, growing, struggling in your understanding of the Bible?* "I was taught a very ... thin strand of belief in the Bible, and I had a negative feeling about [it]. I remember things about people who seemed to believe, and in their lives was that thing called God, and a book called the Bible, and [it] wasn't very strong and lacked a lot of explanations and [caused] a lot of conflict." *Do you want to say anything about the whole process?* "I guess how hard it is to come up with a reason. It means a lot of insight ... to a degree, the amount of frustration and turmoil I go through to make any decision ... some understanding of myself."

Summary and Table

Betty's perspective of faith demonstrates her ability to perceive, understand, and accept multiplicity. This is perhaps the distinguishing feature of perspective B. This interpreting style identifies what is useful or workable for the interpreter, but it is not necessarily applicable to anyone else. Betty is a bargainer in the sense that the Bible may have ultimate authority for her, but she will not impose that understanding on anyone else. She will explore various traditions (including religious traditions other than her own) with interest, respect, and self-reflection. Biblical images, messages, guidelines, and meanings are pondered in terms of their meaningfulness for Betty, and although she might suspect or hope that there is an unshakable truth to be discovered, she will not impose evaluative criteria on someone else's meaning. That's the bargain! Table 4 organizes and summarizes the distinctive features of Bargaining Betty's perspective of faith on biblical interpretation.

Table 4
Betty's Faith Perspective on Biblical Interpretation

Subject Area	Betty's Faith Perspective
World	Multiplistic; centered on interpersonal relationships, one's preferences for diversity
Reasoning	Abstract, hypothetical; imitates analytical process, not clearly separated from feelings. Aware of diversity
Symbol	Has multiple meanings; refers to an abstract reality to which it is bound. A bonding with the symbol and its reality through one's feelings and preferences
Authority	Located in one's preferences, which shape how one relates to external and absolute authority
Self-understanding	World affects individual; individual not agent of change on others or the world; live and let live. Capable of internal change
Interpreting style	Focuses on abstract messages and guidelines that are personally useful but not necessarily useful for others
Authority of the Bible	Located in one's personal feelings or preferences in relating to an external absolute; tacit and multiplistic
Tradition	An affectional aggregation; a past historical entity; diverse, to be questioned
Images of the Bible	Multidimensional, uncritically apprehended; having different meanings for different people
Truth	Whatever one feels is true; a hidden, abstract, external absolute
Self as interpreter	Attuned to multiplistic world, aware of internal change; accepts diversity

4

Perspective C
CONCEPTUALIZING CHARLES

I guess I would put authority of scripture in the hands of the church — that the church as a continuing institution, or more adequately a set of institutions, has decided through the centuries a variety of ways, and over and over again, that scripture is a common basis.   —Charles₇

Charles's Interpreting Style

When Charles interprets 2 Timothy 3:14–17 (see page 7), he analyzes it and presents his conclusions in abstract concepts of meaning. Charles₁ (male, age 22) analyzes the function of faith and contextualizes as "a problem of language" the possible meaning of scripture as inspired. He assumes responsibility for his own learning by evaluating the text's consistency with other parts of his experience. *What do you feel stands out for you in this biblical text?* "The faith that you have already gotten inside you is the guiding principle, and that scripture, however inspired it may be, should be used to instruct others for salvation for faith in Jesus Christ. I think scripture has been inspired by God. Of course, you get into a problem of language. But I think it should be used in context, in relation to the faith you already had inside you." *How do you feel about the text?* "I could...see how it is useful for my own belief that I have learned and internalized, because I read it and I can identify with it. If it said something else, I'd have to think on that and say, 'Well, is that consistent with the way I feel about it and the way I think, in context with other scriptures as well?' I'd have to analyze it."

Charles₂ (male, age 27) reasons analytically from the evidence to a conclusion that he describes using concepts of "growing" and "completeness." He continues to examine the text for other possible meanings, focusing on the ideas it conveys. *What do you think is the main point of the text?* "I'd be hard put to pick out one main point, because on the one hand the author is encouraging the reader to continue from what you have learned, and yet he also goes on to say that scripture will help you continue to grow. It will help you be complete. I suppose those really aren't two different points, but maybe subpoints of the idea of continue to grow to become more complete." *How do you feel about the text?* "I almost got a feeling of...the idea of look out for things that are wrong and stuff like this. But as I read on, there's so much talk about growth and teaching, the idea of learning — that sort of got rid of that [initial] feeling. It's more of a positive, very alive type of thing that the writer is trying to encourage, not a closed-mindedness."

Charles$_3$ (male, age 33) analyzes what he concludes is the writer's main point and then differentiates his own position, based on literary and historical criteria. *What do you think is the main point of the text?* "The main point, it seems to me, is that the scripture is primary, that it is really all we need, that it is of utmost importance." *What do you think it is all about?*

> I wouldn't take the writer's view of the scripture as kind of the final word or the only word of God. I think scriptures are very important and something that I hold dear to myself, but I think that all the scriptures are not inspired by God, and that we can experience and find God outside of scriptures. So I guess what I would do with the text is to see it as a kind of an injunction for me or as a reminder to me of the importance of scripture....I think much of the Bible is myth, poetry, some of it not very inspired poetry, and I think a lot of it is nationalistic literature, history of a people as they have come to understand themselves, and so I think that [it] is good for study and so forth, but I am not sure that it is inspired or that it could be called profitable.

Charles$_4$ (female, age 38) draws a distinction between his own understanding of the text as "inspired" and a common appropriation of it as "the divine word of God." Then he cites criteria for a rational methodology that searches for a more accurate interpretation. *What do you think is the main point of the text?* "Well, I think this is probably proof-texting for many by saying that the Bible is the divine word of God and it should be regarded accordingly and it is all of...equal value....I think that is the way it is used. That is not where I come out personally. Well, I think the scriptures are inspired, but I don't believe they are dictated by God....There are a good many inconsistencies." *What do you think the text is all about?* "Well, I would say from my own point of view, we do need to study and know scripture, but that includes knowing when it was written, the circumstances of who wrote it, why they wrote it, when they wrote it, a good many other things that have to do with where it came from and what it means. And simply to say that it is all the word of God is not accurate."

Charles's View of the Authority of the Bible

For Charles, the authority of the Bible can be established by a logical process. Authority is internal, in that it arises from an individual's assessment of value. The Bible's authority may also be located in a system, for example, as prescribed by Charles's church or denomination according to the criteria used in that institution's process of selecting and ratifying scriptures.

Charles$_1$ reasons on the basis of the writers' internalized authority ("writing out of conscience") and develops certain criteria for establishing the validity of different claims for authority. He rationally distinguishes biblical writings from others that carry less authority. *What reasons would you give for the authority of the scriptures?*

> The belief that the authors wrote not as if they were dictating God's word, but they were writing out of conscience...in relationship to this faith that they had. Well, as far as authority in one's personal faith, this would stand out differently, say, from romantic writers who are trying to express...romantic feeling and emotion. This book implies that there is something deeper, something that is hitting at the ground of our whole being....But the authority that grants its power is based on the belief that the writers themselves believed in the writing, that it was out of their faith that they wrote.

Charles$_3$ dichotomizes the external authority of God or the church from the internal authority of his own experience. *What reasons would you give to someone for the authority of the scriptures?* "I would have to start with my own experiences and tell them of the ways that scripture has helped me. My argument for the authority of the scripture would have to be its utility in my own life and in other persons' lives, as opposed to some other granting them authority by the church or by an authority or by God."

Charles$_5$ (female, age 41) provides criteria for the universal "validity" of the Bible. *What reasons would you give to someone for the authority of the scriptures?* "Some of the reasons that I might give to someone for the authority of the scriptures would be their validity for all times. I mean, they have...lasted for years and years, decades, generations, in all kinds of situations,...that they speak, are universally translatable."

Charles$_6$ (female, age 40) bases the authority of the Bible in the system of a particular "community" and its "tradition," in contrast with other communities and their traditions. *What reasons would you give to someone for the authority of scripture?* "They would have to do with the fact that these are sacred writings of a given community in which I see myself as being involved, negatively and positively. The authority of scripture would not be for everyone. That is, it probably has more authority for those who stood within the same tradition."

Charles$_7$ (male, age 51) also thinks about authority as existing within systems or institutions. *What reasons would you give to someone for the authority of the scriptures?* "I guess I would put authority of scripture in the hands of the church — that the church as a continuing institution, or more adequately a set of institutions, has decided through the centuries a variety of ways, and over and over again, that scripture is a common basis."

Charles's View of Tradition

Charles understands tradition as meaningful concepts from the past that are connected to or continuous with the present. Charles analyzes the characteristics and claims of traditions and then evaluates whether to incorporate them, discard them, or pass them on to others.

Charles$_8$ (female, age 25) understands tradition as a process of interpretation in which the past and the present interact. *What functions as tradition for you?* "For me, the tradition is more from the whole church — what is passed on has truth in it and is acted upon, reworked, interpreted in light of the culture, the society of that day, which I think God is also guiding, and that is passed on to the next generation, and each generation has to make some decisions about that tradition, what they can keep and throw out."

Charles$_9$ (female, age 32) considers tradition as past history that can be meaningful for the present, if one chooses to "learn from the past." *What functions as tradition for you?*

> I guess when I think of tradition, I think of it in terms of a good base to go from and examine things from....I kind of believe the world changes and society changes, and that what was necessarily the right way of doing things a hundred years ago, we have a different situation to deal with now. But I think you can learn from the past. I think if people really tried to learn from the past, they would not get into trouble that keeps recurring.

Charles$_6$ reflects on tradition as a process of socialization to which he can actively respond in ways that transform both him and tradition. *What functions as tradition for you?* "I see myself as standing within [and] at the end of many interrelated though different traditions." *How do you see yourself in relation to tradition?* "It is those things in which I have been socialized and have formed a part of who I am....But the other way is that we are always in our growth somehow in reaction to what we have learned....The conflict that comes out of that is actually what causes growth."

Charles$_7$ also understands tradition as something to be received and at the same time critically evaluated. *What functions as tradition for you?*

"The whole history of the faith, the history of the Hebrew people, their struggle, their self-understanding, the history of the early church.... The second [point] is that I think we are who we are primarily in terms of our tradition. I don't know who I am apart from my roots, and so the tradition gives me identity, it tells me who I am, it names me." *How do you understand yourself in relation to tradition?* "The first word is gratitude. I stand as recipient. The second is critical — look at it carefully and see if that's the identity I choose." Similarly, Charles$_{10}$ (female, age 32) responds, "I see myself as coming out of whatever heritage or tradition or all the forces that made up my life. I would suppose that from here on, it would depend on whether I decide whether to accept or reject whatever I see that tradition to be."

Charles's Images of the Bible

Charles analyzes stories and symbols for their rational and consistent meanings, which can be abstracted from their biblical contexts. Charles$_7$ uses the concept of "drama" to describe the Bible and then analyzes its usefulness in both personal and institutional contexts. *When you think of the Bible, what pictures, words, or phrases come to mind?* "The main term is the drama of the mighty acts of God and the drama of human beings working out their self-understanding, over and over and over again." *What role does the Bible claim in life?* "Primarily twofold. One, personal resource for meditation, digging into a topic, finding out where other people have traveled that particular road before and getting insight from their journey. But secondarily, institutional, finding it a very helpful common base for working with other people within the church and seminary."

Charles$_{10}$ abstracts "concepts and ideas" from the Bible's "witness" to God's relationship with persons. *When you think of the Bible, what pictures, words, or phrases come to mind?* "Oh, gosh, concepts.... You know, this period of history, words are the concepts and ideas, the incidents..." *What are your feelings or thoughts about the Bible?* "That it is a witness of people and God relating to each other, encountering each other." *What role does the Bible play in your life?* "I go to it to help me encounter God, ... to get ideas on the teachings of God through history ... and how to react to a situation of today. I don't mean that I would go to the Bible to prooftext what should be done but to get an idea or the concept expressed in the situation."

Charles$_{11}$ (male, age 33) distinguishes what is "meaningful" in the Bible from what is "dross" with the help of modern analytical tools. *When you think of the Bible, what words, pictures, phrases come to mind?* "The Bible is full of incredibly meaningful things, words of wisdom, some dross, so maybe work comes to mind in trying to clear some of the dross from the beauty, because at certain times in our development, even in our history of people, we just didn't have certain tools, science in particular, recent methods of historical scholarship."

Charles's Understanding of Truth

Charles chooses to think about what is "valid" rather than what is "true." He determines what is valid by using analysis and rational criteria and by seeking consistency. Charles often dichotomizes truth claims into either/or choices, but the authority to make those choices is internalized as his own moral responsibility.

Charles$_7$ uses "critical judgment" to adjudicate among the multiple truths of individuals' experiences. *Do you find that your understanding of the Bible is true?* "Yeah. True in a sense of adequate. True in a sense of historically appropriate. True in a sense of theologically defensible." *Are understandings of the Bible other than your own true?* "True for them, yes. I have to honor other people's interpretations, as every human being is interpreter of his or her own experience. . . . I think that we have some historical data and some other kinds of critical judgment that [are] available to us to help us sort out among all the truths of scripture, and [allow] us to say some truth is more adequate than others."

Charles$_{12}$ (male, age 24) has difficulty using the word *true* but can refer to the possibility that his or others' understandings of the Bible may be "valid" according to certain criteria. *Do you feel that your understanding of the Bible is true?* "I feel that my understanding is valid, that it is useful, that it is pragmatic, that it is something that affirms me, but I am not sure that it is the end-all. It is such a rich body, such a confused body of words, that I try to be very much open to the fact that my view of it may change one way or the other." *Are understandings of the Bible other than your own true?* "Other understandings have, I think, validity. When they differ from mine, they can still be valid, still be affirming, can still be pragmatic, but it is at that point I don't know whether they are true, because I don't know whether mine are true."

Charles$_{13}$ (male, age 23) is aware of plurality of meanings but is concerned to approach them rationally and systematically, which enables him to assess whether an interpretation is "valid." *Do you feel that your understanding of the Bible is true?* "I would say that my understanding in certain peak areas to a certain extent is true. I know that there are myriad ways of interpreting it." *Are understandings of the Bible other than your own true?* "I think reality is an incredibly complicated thing. I see that the Bible can be interpreted in a whole lot of different ways and that within certain brackets, within certain confines, they are all valid."

Charles's Way of Thinking of Self as Interpreter

Charles understands himself as a rational and reflective interpreter. He takes an analytic posture toward the Bible. He assumes self-imposed responsibility for growing and struggling with new concepts as an agent who clarifies and creates meaning.

Charles$_5$ searches for meaning and rationality through his demythologizing of biblical symbols and his struggle to understand the Bible's complexity. *Are there areas in which you wonder or have deep doubts about the Bible?* "Well, I think that I don't have really deep doubts about it because I... believe that the contradictions that are a part of the Bible are not necessarily important in its interpretation.... Whether the virgin birth occurred or not does not really make any difference to me.... The concept and the symbolism of the virgin birth is what's important." *Do you feel that you are changing, growing, struggling in your understanding of the Bible?* "I think any kind of a growth or a change is a struggle. The struggle is, you know, self-imposed, and it is an exciting struggle.... There's a long way to grow in my understanding of the Bible. And, of course, you know, I think the same scripture is useful in a multitude of ways.

Charles$_6$ rejects belief in "ultimate truth" but is interested in "intellectual wonder" as he interacts with the tradition that, for him, has a shaping power. *Are there areas in which you wonder or have deep doubts about the Bible?* "I suppose wonder would have to do more with intellectual wonder. I would like to do more Bible study to find out why we have invested certain words with such weight that they cause evil things to take place.... But it bothers me to the extent that we believe we are acting out of some sort of higher truth or ultimate truth."

Charles$_7$ focuses on adequacy or "appropriate[ness] to the circumstances" as a criterion for the interpretation and authority of scripture. *Are there areas where you have deep doubts about the Bible?*

> Oh, heavens, yes. There are some passages that are terribly inadequate, and other passages that are terribly boring. I don't have doubts in terms of scripture in terms of the story that it is telling, the story of God's relationship to human beings and the struggle for self-understanding in light of that relationship. I do at times have doubts about whether those particular self-understandings are appropriate to the circumstances of the particular situation, such as today.

Charles$_{14}$ (female, age 32) struggles beyond an absolutist mode of interpretation that is imposed from external authorities, to an analytic mode that he can use to examine a text "for what it has to say" for himself. *Do you feel that you are changing, growing, and struggling in your understanding of the Bible?* "Well, I guess mostly I'm struggling just to read it for what it has to say instead of [its] being all these 'shoulds' and 'shouldn'ts' the way I had been taught. And I hope I'm growing so that I cannot necessarily see just what's written there, but to see what lies behind it."

Charles[15] (male, age 28) is disturbed by concepts that do not make sense to him, but he takes the initiative to struggle with the scriptures in an interactive style of interpretation. *Are there areas in which you wonder or have deep doubts about the Bible?* "Well, the theology of the Old Testament is very disturbing for me. I have a hard time with thinking that punishment and good comes from God. I have a hard time understanding how those folks could justify walking up and killing somebody and saying that is what God wanted them to do. That needs further enlightenment." *Do you feel that you are changing, growing, struggling in your understanding of the Bible, and how?* "Yeah,...as I interact with the scriptures and allow them to speak to me. [At the same time,] I interact with the society, and it prods me to do things that I don't want to do as I interact with God,...and all that will keep me struggling with the scriptures."

Summary and Table

The search for rationality characterizes Charles's perspective of faith. He understands himself as a reasoning and reflective being who takes responsibility for his own growth and creation of meaning. He interprets biblical texts by analyzing images and abstracting concepts that are consistent, clear, and coherent. This might involve using critical procedures developed by various academic disciplines to demythologize symbols and stories in order to obtain interpretations that are appropriate for his contemporary context.

In his search for rational meaning, Conceptualizing Charles also struggles with how people have been confronted by God within the context of different communities and traditions. The determination of authority for Charles is basically an internal, rational process, so he analyzes traditions for their validity and chooses to endorse or transmit those he reasons to be most adequate. Although Charles can assess and understand the rational validity of concepts and theories other than his own, he will often dichotomize those understandings by contrasting and polarizing opposing viewpoints. Table 5 organizes and summarizes the distinctive features of Charles's perspective of faith on biblical interpretation.

Table 5
Charles's Faith Perspective on Biblical Interpretation

Subject Area	Charles's Faith Perspective
World	An explicit, rational system; centered on rationality, concepts, ideologies
Reasoning	Abstract, analytical, reflective, dichotomized. Searches for rationality, consistency, coherence; knows intellectual passion and wonder
Symbol	Rationally separated from the conceptual reality to which it refers. Rational but passionate bonding to the conceptual reality
Authority	Located in the system and its credentialed representatives, in logically determined truth; also internalized within the individual
Self-understanding	Self is agent of change, capable of affecting world. Conscious of internal change
Interpreting style	Analytical, uses abstract concepts of meaning
Authority of the Bible	Located in the system and/or in truth as logically determined by the individual
Tradition	Abstract meanings; historical past connected to present; to be analyzed and evaluated
Images of the Bible	Abstract concepts of meaning and images
Truth	Ideas "valid" rather than "true," determined by use of analysis, rational criteria, consistency; rational relativism
Self as interpreter	Rational and reflective. Feels self-imposed responsibility for growth and creation of meaning

5

Perspective D:
DIALECTICAL DONNA

*The authority of the scripture comes out of an authoritative vision
and intention on the part of all the writers of the scripture...about
the relationship of persons to God and to one another in the search
for meaning and understanding of life's experiences and questions.*

— Donna₃

Donna's Interpreting Style

When Donna interprets 2 Timothy 3:14–17 (see page 7), she analyzes it
and dialogues with it for the disclosure of images, ideas, and new meanings
that can be integrated into her self-understanding and personal commitment. Donna₁ (female, age 33) demonstrates this very effectively with her
critical self-awareness of different, almost contradictory meanings she can
discover in a single text. *What do you think is the main point of the text?*
"I guess, for me, that by being aware of what we have learned and from
whom we learned it and what the instructions are — they are valuable —
and therefore, we may be complete if we follow those things and act on
them." *Do you agree or disagree, and why?*

> There are a few phrases in it [that] I have trouble with. Yet, when I
> go beyond just my first reaction to them, I at least can appreciate even
> those.... The phrase that first struck me wrong was "for reproof." I
> heard that as being critical. "You aren't doing it right. That is the way
> you ought to do it." Yet, when I go beyond that, I think of the essence
> of discipline and discipleship and appreciate that as a part of [it]. That
> is the way I would interpret "for reproof, for correction."

Donna₂ (female, age 38) makes reference to a similar dialectic that she
experiences with the Bible as a "sparring partner." *What do you feel stands
out for you in this text?* "I guess that although I am not a believer in biblical inerrancy or that kind of thing, I have found the Bible, its stories and
messages, to be about the most helpful sparring partner that I have had

since I was ten years old. I have been going back and forth since that time and find it to be a very helpful dimension." *How do you feel about the text? Do you agree or disagree?* "The concept of canon is important to me, so just because I don't particularly like one passage, I would not prefer that it be cut out of the Bible. I would rather that it be there and scratched me occasionally. Maybe at some point it will be helpful."

Donna$_3$ (female, age 34) analyzes and integrates both abstract ("as a learner") and personal ("my understanding") meanings from the text. She enlarges her interpretation to include several types of communities. *What stands out for you in this biblical text?* "I think as a learner I am engaged in learning continually, and I learn as a member of a specific faith community and as a member of another kind of community, which I guess I would call a societal community. All of those different areas of my life integrate to give me a sense of being a part of all human endeavor." *Please summarize what the text is all about,* "I think the text is calling on me to consider the validity of the roots of my tradition, my own understanding of ministry of service and what I think it is all about...and how I go about using that tradition as a part of my understanding of what ministry is."

Donna$_4$ (male, age 31) also describes interpretation as an interactive relationship with a text that is fluid ("malleable") but coherent ("foundation," "structure"), not haphazard. *How do you feel about the text?*

> Well, to me it has a really nice flavor, probably because of my child-hood and background. There were times when I thought it was pretty ridiculous to participate in some of the things that I was taught, and yet the older I got, the more I was [convinced] that it was really sound stuff, solid foundational stuff with which I could build in my own structure — all those persons who were in my life who helped me lay a foundation, you know, who have given me that foundation so that I can continue to learn in what I have been taught, what I really believe. It has become very malleable, the structure. It changes, depending on my life situation, but the foundation stays the same, so I've got a really good feeling about it.

Donna's View of the Authority of the Bible

The authority of the Bible is partial for Donna, in that she relates it to other authorities (e.g., tradition, reason, experience) that are weighed in a dialectical process. Donna internalizes the Bible's authority in a personal and contextualized commitment that is grounded in her experience. At the same time, her experience is given shape by the framework of history and community. The Bible's authority is of a type that evokes participation in and commitment to a new reality.

Donna$_3$ locates the Bible's authority in the writers' internal integration of

"understanding," "experience," "rational beliefs," and "vision" of meaning in relation to God and community. *What reason would you give to
someone for the authority of the scriptures?*

> The authority of the scripture comes out of an authoritative vision
> and intention on the part of all the writers of the scripture who [were]
> inspired by their understanding, their experience, their rational beliefs
> about and their vision of what it means to be engaged in an active
> life of faith in relationship with God within a community, a particu-
> lar community of faith. The intention is to say something about the
> relationship of persons to God and to one another in the search for
> meaning and understanding of life's experiences and questions.

Donna₄ "give[s] the Bible authority" because she perceives several kinds
of authority interacting to both represent and produce particular meanings. *What reasons would you give to someone for the authority of the
scriptures?*

> The Bible has authority, and I give the Bible authority.... There was
> authority going on in all those stories, you know, man's authority,
> God's authority over persons, women's authority. There was just au-
> thority there in terms of the interaction they all had with one another.
> Also, I give authority because of... the tradition of the Bible, going
> back into oral tradition.... They had authority of symbol in that they
> evoked certain kinds of dimensions going on inside a person, evoked
> certain kinds of images. So the Bible to me has tremendous authority,
> just because of the people who have participated in the history of it.

Donna₅ (male, age 44) bases scripture's authority in her own integration
of reason and experience rather than in an absolutist understanding of the
Bible as rules and examples. *What reasons would you give to someone for
the authority of scripture?*

> One of the reasons that I would *not* give is the fact that they have
> been in existence for such a long time and this is a law and they
> are unbendable. I would try to relate the authority to... what they
> have meant to me in my living, how they have helped me, and per-
> haps how they have hindered me. I would [ask] the person... "Is
> what the scriptures say reasonable to you?"... I would encourage
> them to seek something out of their own experience that would have
> meaning to that. I would impress on them that they are part of the
> long tradition of the church. They have worked before; they can
> come alive because the scriptures deal with the basic human prob-
> lems of loneliness, anxiety, ambiguity. The scriptures... replay how
> man throughout time has faced these problems of being human and
> recognizing [his] creatureliness.

Donna₆ (female, age 56) locates authority in people's shared experiences and meaning, rather than in something external and absolute. *What reasons would you give to someone for the authority of scriptures?*

> One would be that the scriptures do come out of people's experiences of God. I tend to place trust in people when they explain and interpret their experiences. This would lend an authority to it, just as if I would tell you a meaningful experience in my life. . . . Also, the fact that the scriptures have spoken in very meaningful ways to people through thousands of years. I have some problems with the word *authority*. I do not like to see it used in an absolute way.

Donna's View of Tradition

For Donna, tradition consists of the particular traditions of the past and the universal human experiences with which persons understand themselves to be integrated emotionally, rationally, and aesthetically. Donna₁ thinks of tradition as things from the past with which she has a meaningful personal bond. She also conveys how dynamic that relationship is for her. *What functions as tradition for you?* "Tradition [is] things which come out of the past and which have taken on meaning for me: reading the Bible stories together as a family, sharing with other people in a variety of celebrations, both in worship and in the festivity. They are very old and ancient traditions which have come through and have been filtered in and out of our culture." *How do you understand yourself in relation to that tradition?* "I am an integral part of it. For that tradition to function, I have to interact with it; otherwise it doesn't function for me. It also has a little bit to do with the sharing of traditions and teaching into the future so that others will share my tradition."

Donna₅ observes that traditions have validity for persons who can connect their experiences with the time-tested interpretations that have been passed down through the years. *What functions as tradition for you?*

> Tradition to me means finding the original formula, perhaps reevaluating it in the light of our present experiences and culture, and bringing it forth into a meaningful relation. . . . It is that I can look back thousands of years when the Bible was written and say those things that I see are meaningful for me because they come out of my experience. I also experience them. They sound reasonably correct. Traditionally, they have been lifted and brought forth and survived each generation. They have been tested and used. Therefore, I give them greater validation because they are things that have come out of time and survived.

Donna's Images of the Bible

Images of the Bible for Donna evoke feelings and raise questions, engaging her in that she is personally confronted by God within the context of community and traditions. She regards the Bible as subject rather than object, confronting her with questions and new meanings that she appropriates in terms of personal commitment.

Donna$_3$ includes both individual and communal images of the Bible in her attempt to capture the transcendent quality of one's encounter with God. *What pictures, words, or phrases come to mind when you think of the Bible?* "Vision, picture of a person apprehended by some knowing of some kind of ultimate reality. I think of the Bible as a story of the journey of many, many individuals who are engaged in asking questions about the source and quality of life and being."

Donna$_4$ reflects on the changes in her approach to the Bible, which she now views appreciatively for its testimony to our human struggle to create meaning. *When you think of the Bible, what pictures, words, or phrases come to mind?* "All the Bible is really is people, humankind's script of how we have and continue to relate to one another, the problems we have with one another and about the earth, and the problems we have with this transcendent God." *What are your thoughts and feelings about the Bible?*

> I was never really able to get into the Bible because I had so many mental blocks and the roadblocks were set up. And now I have a very deep respect for the Bible, because it records human history, human struggle, people in search of something better, people in search of the lost chord, in search of that transcendent God, and the revealing truth that God is real.... It is affirming to life, affirming to growth, and affirming to individual dignity and individual rights, and all of that.

Donna$_7$ (male, age 25) uses individual and community images to talk about the Bible's meaning. She clearly distinguishes thought from feeling but employs them both in several levels of interaction with the text. *What pictures, words, or phrases come to mind when you think about the Bible?* "I kind of see a picture of an individual feeling confronted.... There is a need to rethink some things or do some things, make some action.... But also...the story is being told to other people. Even if it is a story of that confrontation, it is a story with people listening. So it is individual and community images I see." *What are your feelings or thoughts about the Bible?*

> I feel a sense of comradeship with the Bible, because it expresses part of the experience of God that people have had.... When I think about the Bible, separated from feelings,...intellectually I have to keep in mind that there is a history of the tradition. There is a trajectory of meaning going on that I need to be aware of.... The feeling level [is

that] there is a relationship going on between my experience and the experience the Bible gives witness to. There is an interchange back and forth.

Donna₆ joins feelings with ideas in relating her confrontations with the Bible as a subject rather than an object to be deciphered. *When you think of the Bible, what pictures, words, or phrases come to mind?* "All these people and different experiences and kinds of situations in a vivid picture, almost like a time line, except it has a depth to it." *What are your feelings or thoughts about the Bible?* "It helps us to interpret ourselves. Much of my life has been related to experiences in the Bible. Usually when I have really dug in and worked with a particular text intensely, then it speaks to me. It is some sort of living kind of thing that speaks to me, and I can dialogue."

Donna's Understanding of Truth

Donna understands truth as rooted in history and community and as that to which she is committed at a particular moment in her life. What is "true" for Donna has been consciously chosen and integrated from among many choices and by the use of different kinds of criteria. She makes her commitments in the expectation that they may change and grow in differing life situations. For Donna, the word *true* is problematic and requires definition. There is always more to consider.

Donna₃ rejects an absolutist and monolithic understanding of the word *true*, choosing instead to identify a dynamic process that draws from multiple experiences and perceptions of truth among people and within herself over time. *Do you feel your understanding of the Bible is true?*

> True? . . . Well, I think there are many ways to understand, to interpret the truth contained in the Bible, and my particular interpretation or understanding won't be the same [as that] of someone struggling with the text out of a different life situation or given a different perspective. To me it is a really dynamic process that goes on between the person reading the scripture and what has been set down by writers out of another time and another perspective. There is not an absolute truth which if we just have the right key we could open . . . questions would go away. . . . I don't think that is the way truth is. Truth depends for its truth on many perspectives. . . . My feeling is that my particular understanding of the Bible is meaningful for me, and that changes with time and my own learning. . . . Many understandings of the Bible are true, but truth is a relative category.

Donna₇ reflects on the meaning of *true* in terms of her particular personal commitment within a wider communal context. *Do you feel your understanding of the Bible is true?*

The word that sticks out in that statement is *true*. It is true for me at this time and place in my life, my understandings of how things are and all that. I think that this understanding is within tolerable limits of the understanding of the Christian community at large of what the Bible is and how it functions, but there is not any one true understanding. Mine changes and the community's changes, but right now that is where it is and I have to act on it.

Donna$_6$ brings rational examination and intuition together to bear on her unfolding understanding of truth. *Do you feel that your understanding of the Bible is true?* "I would say that I feel my understandings are grounded in a lot of discipline and study. Also, my understandings come through intuition and metaphorical kinds of things. I wake up in the morning with more understandings. It is a very true thing with me, although my understanding of it changes."

Donna's Way of Thinking of Self as Interpreter

Donna understands herself as an interpreter who engages others, including the Bible, as responsible and worthy subjects. She treats persons equally as dialogue partners who are capable of commitment and change. She has the ability to evaluate and integrate her own thinking and acting in terms of her commitments.

Donna$_3$ self-consciously grants validity to the Bible because of its particular significance for the coherent meaning she makes of life. *Are there areas in which you wonder or have doubts about the Bible?*

I am very much aware of the fact that as a body of tradition, as a locus of questioning, as a source that is germane to my own particular faith tradition, I have no doubts that it is valid. It phrases for me an understanding of life and meaning and value that gives me coherence. . . . The Bible is full of contradictions, because it is a human document. It is a story about the struggle that human beings have in trying to understand and articulate their ultimate concern and some understanding of God.

Donna$_4$ places herself with others in a continual process of interpretation and evaluation. She has a dialectical style of holding contrary parts together for the purpose of rich dialogue, the outcome of which is growth and renewed commitment. *Do you feel that you are changing, growing, struggling in your relation to the Bible?*

Sure I am. Every time I pick it up and read it . . . there's a challenge to me as to my interpretation. . . . The Bible is a piece of interpretation by all the people who put it together, and all the people who lived lives surrounding the events that took place, to bring other people to the place of wanting to write it. It has all been interpretation, and so I have to be involved continually in an interpretative process in relation to life all the time....I have to be continually evaluating, which means I have to continue to be open enough to see contradictions and hold them in some kind of tension....I just hold them in abeyance and dialogue about them and get further information. Even the things I have come to decision about, say these are true and these are untrue, I even have to hold in a place that allows dialogue, because if I don't continue to dialogue, how will I grow?

Donna[7] also sees herself as an active participant in an ongoing conversation with the Bible. She distinguishes and affirms another way of interpreting the Bible ("literally") as an example of a healthy challenge for her that keeps her faith alive and growing. She understands herself as living in the paradox between "conserving" and pushing forward. *Are there areas in which you wonder or have deep doubts about the Bible?* "For me, the interaction with the Bible, the interaction with faith and God, is very important. It keeps me alive. I would be very worried if I thought I had the answers to everything and had it all wrapped up. It's nice to have a little more certainty than it is to have doubt, but it isn't necessary all the time, and sometimes it isn't healthy." *Do you feel that you are growing, changing, struggling in your understanding of the Bible?*

> The main thing that challenges me about the Bible is that in the tradition, there have been an awful lot of people who have taken things literally....That literal kind of interpretation often gets pushed to the wayside and yet always comes back to challenge me....I expect that my understandings are going to change. I have a conserving thing going and a pushing-me-forward kind of thing going at the same time. That is a tension that doesn't let me get too comfortable.

Summary and Table

Donna's perspective of faith integrates feeling and reasoning with personal commitment. It is important to her to examine and articulate her location in a pluralistic and relativistic world. In her movement toward integrative thinking, she embraces ambiguity, complexity, and paradox as much as rationality. Donna cherishes dialogue with the Bible and with other persons as subjects or partners with whom she discovers new meanings. Within the larger context of communities and traditions, she experiences a personal confrontation with God through her engagement with diverse images, stories, and analysis of biblical texts.

Dialectical Donna understands herself in both continuity and discontinuity with traditions. The past is part of her, yet she takes responsibility for evaluating her past in terms of the aspects of her traditions that she will appropriate into her present commitments. Similarly, the Bible has authority for Donna, but she weighs its authority along with other kinds of authorities as she determines where she will stand within a relativistic world and within her community of faith. Truth is what Donna is committed to today, based upon how she examines data, what has been tested in history and community, and what makes sense of her particular personal and social life situation. Table 6 organizes and summarizes the distinctive features of Donna's faith perspective on biblical interpretation.

Table 6
Donna's Faith Perspective on Biblical Interpretation

Subject Area	Donna's Faith Perspective
World	A pluralistic, ambiguous, or complex unity; centered on vision, integration, basic rights. Can stand outside a system
Reasoning	Abstract, dialectical, paradoxical; moving toward integration. Has critical self-awareness
Symbol	Joined with the reality and one's feelings and ideas into a new vision. Emotional-rational-aesthetic bonding
Authority	Located in the weighing of traditional authorities in a dialectical process; internalized
Self-understanding	Egalitarian; all persons capable of dialogue and effecting change; mutual respect for persons as ends and not means
Interpreting style	Analytical, uses abstract concepts of meaning; integrates new meanings with personal commitment
Authority of the Bible	Partial, weighing with other traditional authorities in a dialectical process; ultimate, internalized in personal commitment
Tradition	Integration of past; universal and personal; emotional-rational-aesthetic bonding
Images of the Bible	Abstract and personal; personal confrontation with God within the context of community and traditions; subject rather than object
Truth	Examined, rooted in history and community; that to which one is committed today
Self as interpreter	Dialogues with Bible and others as equal subjects; evaluates and integrates thinking and feeling, personal commitment

6

HOW PERSPECTIVES
ACTUALLY WORK

*We are many selves acting as one.... Pluralism [is a] metaphor for
psychological processes.*   —Andrew Samuels[1]

Although we have described four perspectives as composite types, each
with its own unique characteristics, rarely would one find a person who
perfectly represents one of these types. The results of our research show
that almost all of our subjects responded to the Biblical Interview out of
two or occasionally three perspectives, depending on the concept or topic
they were discussing. Our work with the perspectives in various groups
of adults over the past decade has confirmed these observations. To think
of "mixed perspectives" seems to us to be far more representative of the
complexities of human life than to imagine that people always consistently
interpret their life experiences from one general vantage point.

There could be several reasons for disparities in how one thinks about
different areas of his or her life. It is important to consider some of these
as they impact our normative expectations for mature and competent adult
functioning. But first, to illustrate the tensions and transitions that commonly intermingle in mixed perspectives, we present excerpts from two
Biblical Interviews. The topical areas are the same as those described in
the previous four chapters, and each response is followed by an abbreviated reference or "pointer" to similarities with one of the four perspectives.
These are our evaluations of the data. Readers might want to refer to
the perspective descriptions in the previous chapters and make their own
judgments about these two interviews. Remember that the *structure* of our
thinking is always cloaked in the fabric of *content,* and the difficult task
is to uncover the framework that provides the shape of meaning for our
experiences.

---

1. Andrew Samuels, *The Plural Psyche* (London: Routledge, 1989), 3.

June: Perspectives C and D

June is the imaginary name we will use for a thirty-year-old woman who responds to the questions of the Biblical Interview out of faith perspectives C (Conceptualizing Charles) and D (Dialectical Donna).

June's Interpreting Style

June is consistent in using perspective C, with some perspective D, as her in-terpreting style. *What stands out for you in this biblical text?* "The process . . . God's involvement in history, in the sacred writings. God's involvement in the individuals' lives and preparing for ministry from the time they were children." *What do you think is the main point of the text?* "That we are a part of the historical body . . . that there has been involvement all along and this is just one point and perhaps the culmination of history with Christ coming, the Jesus Christ event." Perspective C uses abstract concepts of meaning, such as "God's involvement in history" and "the Jesus Christ event."

How do you feel about the text? Do you agree or disagree? "I agree with it mainly because I have seen the journey in my own history and involvement of God in my own salvation, in my own movement toward ministry." Perspective D demonstrates a critical self-awareness and personal commitment.

Would you please summarize what you think the text is all about. "The text is saying there are some very concrete, historically verifiable things that have happened that indicate God's faithfulness and God's action toward his people. Those things have been set down in sacred writings. They have been taught orally, and we are part of that tradition." In addition to abstracting concepts such as "God's action toward his people," perspective C appeals to what is "verifiable."

June's View of the Authority of the Bible

June's reasoning about the authority of the Bible reflects perspective C. *What reasons would you give to someone for the authority of the scrip-tures?* "I don't see the authority as being necessarily the words themselves but that they are an accurate record of the history of the traditions, the myths, of God's involvement in history, of his specific relationship with the people of Israel." For perspective C, authority is based in logically determined truth ("accurate record").

June's View of Tradition

June thinks about tradition using perspectives C and D. *What functions as tradition for you?*

There are a number of things. Some of them are very Catholic: re-ligious communities, the experiences of the desert, the desert fathers and others, the devotional life, the historical church which built upon the basic writings and always refers back to them. The combination of the historical and personal event of Jesus that can be set in a historical content and context, and can also be experienced personally and has been throughout history by those people who consider themselves to be believers.

Perspective D uses a dialectical style ("combination...set in a historical content and context") and integrates ideas ("the historical and personal event of Jesus"), feelings ("experienced personally"), and the personal ("people who consider themselves to be believers").

How do you understand yourself in relation to tradition? "I guess I believe that I have a lot to learn from those people who have been great believers throughout the ages....The experiences that these people had are available to me, so particularly [in regard to] those having to do with spiritual life and devotional life, the tradition is very, very important — it is part of having roots, and it is part of not losing one's way." Perspective C understands tradition in terms of abstract meanings from the past ("spiritual life and devotional life"), but elements of perspective D are indicated by the choice to locate the tradition within a personal history ("available to me...having roots...not losing one's way").

What is more important to you, the Bible or tradition? "Oh, I don't think I could separate them, because I think tradition has always been informed by the Bible, and I see very little in tradition that I value that does not also have its roots in the Bible, and I don't think either the tradition or the Bible should be worshiped but are both a witness to who God is and how God has become manifest in human history." Perspective C reasons for consistency ("tradition has always been informed by the Bible") and separates ideas from the symbols of tradition and Bible ("[both are] a witness to who God is and how God has become manifest in history").

June's Images of the Bible

Perspectives C and D are reflected in June's responses about images of the Bible. *When you think of the Bible, what pictures, words, or phrases come to mind?* "Something very much alive, fallible, people making mistakes, constantly bringing people back to himself, a lot of mystery, a lot of things in it I don't like, that I don't understand." *What are your feelings or thoughts about the Bible?* "To me now, the Bible is more of a record of God's movement in history, but also more like a window through which we can begin to see some of the life of the Spirit and God can become real to us. It is a means of revelation rather than a collection of revealed writings." In addition to a rational description of the writings, perspective D views the Bible as subject ("something very much alive," "like a window through which...God can become real to us") and thinks about the Bible dialectically as something valuable but also problematic ("alive" yet "fallible," "bringing people back" but having "things in it I don't like").

What role does the Bible play in your life?

> I study it because I want to understand exactly what was being said at that time, what those words meant to the people who heard them, so that I can have as accurate a picture as possible of what the writings mean. I think that the ethical values that have come down to us are based on the Bible and are meant to be based on many of the larger principles in the Bible, and I do tend to ignore some of the other things that I tend to believe are culturally biased. I don't know that is being terribly consistent, but I have a little trouble with the apostle Paul sometimes.

Perspective C searches for rationality, consistency, analysis ("so that I can have as accurate a picture as possible"). June's response could represent perspective D, with the references to "larger principles" and "ethical values" indicating something of her personal commitment.

June's Understanding of Truth

June understands truth from perspectives C and D. *Do you feel that your understanding of the Bible is true?* "I hope so. I think that I am very open to anything that is there, anything that could be called fact, and I am also very open to being spoken to, to being in the presence of God and letting the Spirit speak to me, but I also realize that no person is in possession of the whole truth, and nobody has an accurate picture." Perspective C searches for "fact" and "an accurate picture." Perspective D understands that truth involves "being spoken to" in personal confrontation and that symbols are partial and ambiguous (no one has "the whole truth"). *Are understandings of the Bible other than your own true?*

> Yes, I think so. Because not any one person...my experience is limited. I am going to interpret a lot of what is said by my own experience....I am limited in my understanding by my experience, by the fact that I am a finite human being and that other people are also, but they might understand part of it in a different way and perhaps just a different dimension of something that I see only one dimension of.

Perspective C uses rational criteria to construct a theory of rational relativism ("they might understand part of it in a different way"). Combining rational criteria with personal "experience" may indicate a transition to perspective D.

June's Way of Thinking of Self as Interpreter

June reflects on herself as an interpreter using perspectives C and D. *Are there areas in which you wonder or have deep doubts about the Bible?*

"Yes, sometimes I do. I wonder about why some things are in it, why the accounts of Yahweh slaughtering the enemies of Israel are there.... Sometimes I wonder about the things that are used, have been used in various times to promote slavery, to promote sexism, racism, all those." Perspective C reflects a search for rational consistency.

What is your understanding of how the Bible came to be? "I think it developed over a period of time into what it is now.... I think that the general meaning behind those events or those traditions [is] consistent. Sometimes the details really vary, but I guess there is something consistent coming across, yet the Spirit of God can speak through the Bible now." Perspective D includes reasoning toward what is "consistent" (perspective C) as well as an understanding of the Bible as subject through which "the Spirit of God can speak."

Do you feel that you are changing, growing, struggling in your understanding of the Bible?

> Yes, definitely. Well, coming from a background where the Bible was considered to be right next to God, probably on the other side of Jesus, you know, it is hard sometimes to be in a place where people are saying, "Well, that is just a metaphor, those are just discrepancies," or, "That really didn't happen," or "That was put in the mouths of so and so." So it is sometimes hard for me to hear some of those things, yet I don't want to be afraid of learning facts. I also don't want to let other persons' opinions color what really should be coming through, either. I think I will always struggle with that, but I think I will always have a very strong respect for the Bible because of my background, because of the emphasis that was put on it, because I suspect that I will always be in dialogue with people with those same religious views.

Perspective D is indicated by June's ability to recognize and take the role of other groups with whom she disagrees.

Harry: Perspective B (with Some A and C)

In the following responses, a twenty-eight-year-old man whom we'll call Harry interprets, for the most part, out of perspective B. In a few instances, however, he interprets concepts and issues from perspective A and perspective C.

Harry's Interpreting Style

Harry's interpreting style basically represents perspective B, with some perspective A. *What do you think is the main point of the text?* "Basically, I would say that it wants you to know that what you have learned in the past is very important. It also wants you to know that what you will be learning in the future and currently adds to that. You established a foundation to this point, and you should use that foundation throughout the rest of your life." Perspective A focuses on the message of the Bible, or what "it wants you to know," and seems to attribute to it an absolute authority ("foundation").

What do you feel about the text? "I agree with it, because I see that is what has happened in my life. It has been affirmed in my life. It is exactly how it is." Perspective B appeals to a concept of workability ("it has been affirmed") for appropriating what a text says.

Would you summarize what you think the text is all about?

> The foundations are very important, and you should continue to build upon [them]. It also uses all the tools that you learned in that growing-up period to, again, add to your life. You shouldn't discount them even though some of them are bad and some of them are good. Basically, the point is that the Bible is something that is constantly in use, one of those tools. It is something that should be used.

Perspective B refers to the applicability or usefulness of the Bible ("you should continue to build upon [it]," "add to your life") and acknowledges multiple meanings ("some...bad and some...good").

Harry's View of the Authority of the Bible

Harry uses perspective B in his way of thinking about the authority of the Bible. *What reasons would you give someone for the authority of scripture?* "I have been in places where it has been absolutely impossible for me to get across my understanding of how the Bible is an authority for me. But, the Bible is an authority for other people in a different understanding. If I can find out about their understandings and how that relates to them, then I can use that and show them how the Bible is their authority as well." Perspective B accepts "different" understandings (i.e., a multiplicity) of authority.

Harry's View of Tradition

Harry's way of thinking about tradition reflects perspectives A and B. *What functions as tradition for you?* "Tradition functions for me in the fact that human beings have an existence.... It's like our roots. If we don't have any existence, then the human being is cut off from other human beings. Tradition therefore comes through as our root structure for other human beings.... They are in it all the time. So, tradition becomes changeable and sometimes bad as well as good." Perspective B detects multiple possibilities in tradition ("changeable...sometimes bad as well as good").

What kinds of traditions function in your life?

> Basically...education....Church is a tradition....Tradition functions as an order for my life. My parents taught me certain things

that I still perceive in my life. . . . see difference in other people, too, so I don't put that tradition on other people. I use the things they taught me, the traditions, for things that I see that help, not in my understanding, but in my relationships with other people. You know, be nice, be courteous. . . . Those are traditions for me.

Perspective B understands and accepts "difference in other people," although the traditions cited here are the good intentions and actions characteristic of perspective A.

Harry's Images of the Bible

Harry's way of imaging the Bible reflects perspective B, with some C. *When you think of the Bible, what pictures, words, or phrases come to mind?* "Oh, uh, basically I would go back to my childhood of stories of Jesus, Moses parting the Red Sea, this kind of stuff. In my latter years, say five years, I have been more perceptive of the stories of Jesus and the relationships that he had with other people. Those things and the things he said and the things the other people said have become more important in my life and more of something I will use." With perspective B, Harry focuses on usefulness ("something I will use"), but he describes the Bible's content in terms of abstract concepts of meaning ("stories," "relationships"), which is characteristic of perspective C.

What are your feelings and thoughts about the Bible?

The Bible, to me, is more a source of a heck of a lot of people's writings that are true today as much as they were for the time that they were written. If we can understand why they were written, what pattern they were written in, and the culture they were written in, and who it was that was writing them and their understandings of what their life and traditions were, then I think we can understand it. The Bible is more — if I didn't have the Bible, I would have more of a loss to try to answer some of the questions I have.

Harry begins using perspective C in describing a rational or critical methodology for interpreting the Bible, but he concludes with a perspective A or B view of authority by appealing to the Bible as an "answer" book.

Harry's Understanding of Truth

Harry's way of understanding truth reflects perspective B. *Do you feel that your understanding of the Bible is true?*

That gets into my understanding of the Bible, because again, my perception of the Bible is how I interpret it. Other people's interpretation might be different than mine. . . . So, my interpretation becomes right for me, because I see how it has entered into my life. But it is something I will try to get across to other people, but I will not put it on other people that this is the only way that you will ever be saved or know the Bible.

In thinking from perspective B, Harry is aware of "different" interpretations but "will not put" his interpretation on other people as "the only way" to be saved.

Harry's Way of Thinking of Self as Interpreter

Harry uses perspective B in thinking about himself as an interpreter. *Are there areas of the Bible in which you have deep doubts or wonder about the Bible?*

> Yes. Book of Revelations [*sic*] is one of them. Some of the things in Job are a little peculiar. It isn't that I don't understand them. Some of the interpretations that other people put upon them I don't see in those writings. . . . I don't see that there is a great deal in the Bible, uh, there are always new things coming up for me that I have read before but [it] still comes up with a different interpretation.

Perspective B is aware of different interpretations but is not concerned to make them consistent.
Do you feel that you are changing, growing, struggling in your understanding of the Bible?

> Yes. . . . I think that each time I read a passage out of the Bible, I will spend a great deal of time going over it and over it and over it. Then I will put it away, and maybe five years from now I will come back to the same passages. Through the growing that I have done in those five years, I will perceive that passage being different. So, for me, the Bible is something that is a reference, and yet it is a constantly changing reference.

Harry understands "growing" in terms of perceiving a "passage being different," which reflects the multiplistic character of perspective B.

Observations

When we think of Christian diversity, we usually think of different opinions or viewpoints *among* people. These interviews with June and Harry remind us that there is actually "diversity" *within* people also. It is overly simplistic to think of a person as always consistent. Our feelings, thoughts, and activities bespeak the multiplicity that we must constantly formulate into some coherence that gives us meaning and a sense of personal identity. Mary Catherine Bateson refers to this activity as improvisation, or "that act of creation that engages us all — the composition of our lives."[2] Perspectives of faith indicate the ways that persons are "composing" meaning. The presence of mixed perspectives in many people is another important reason to avoid labeling people or putting them into boxes of predictability. We should not overlook the fact that mixed perspectives may provide a basis for discovering common ground in areas of conflict between persons. The human interpreter is a rich and complex phenomenon, and faith is a *dynamic* process.

As we reflected on the presence of mixed perspectives in our research, we identified a process that we call "encapsulation." Apparently, different contexts or topic areas can evoke different ways of thinking within a single person. Often, emotionally laden content is expressed through a significantly different structure or perspective. The majority of the interview responses clustered within a cohesive structure. However, a few were strikingly disparate, as though a different person were speaking!

One subject expressed an understanding of law similar to Conceptualizing Charles's perspective: "The laws, at least in this country, are made by those in authority, with the common consent of the people, for the most part.... We have the responsibility to each other in holding up agreements we have between each other."[3] Reasoning about the common good and the consensus of people living together in a society is characteristic of Charles's attention to systems and abstract concepts. However, when the topic turns to religious concepts such as sin and God, the person being interviewed responds differently:

> I feel that [if] Heinz had to go to the extent of doing something sinful, then his motives were wrong in the first place, and that may be a little difficult to follow, but I believe that God would have control over the situation quite a bit.... I think if Heinz prays about it, tries to work out a way to get this drug, and would have to resort to some sort of sin to get it, then I should say he should not.

This response is more like that of Affiliating Al, who would be concerned about the person's intentions and would focus on God's absolute authority. Another interview shows religious concepts used in two very different ways. The subject states,

> There are some laws men create that may inadvertently be against God's law, and you may find yourself having to break that.... I would follow the higher law of God. God's laws are ultimately for the good

---

2. Mary Catherine Bateson, *Composing a Life* (New York: Atlantic Monthly Press, 1989), 1.

3. In this and the following interview excerpts, the subjects are responding to Kohlberg's "Moral Dilemma 3," more commonly known as the Heinz dilemma. For more information about the interviews, see appendix B.

of all; I am not convinced that a lot of laws made by men are for the good of all people but [are] more...for a particular group of people.

Conceptualizing Charles might also use the concept of higher laws that human laws can add to but cannot displace. However, when the same person just quoted introduces intentions and feelings into our conversation, there is a marked change in structure: "If Heinz had stolen the drug and had the attitude that it was correct and that he could see nothing wrong with breaking the law,...that he had a feeling of contrition, that he was human, that he had to save his wife's life,...I would as a judge go along with it." Although the outcome is the same, the latter response sounds more like Affiliating Al, who might make decisions on the basis of feelings and intentions rather than on an analysis of a greater good.

These examples are brief and are taken out of their interview context; nevertheless, they convey one type of diversity we find in adults, especially with regard to religious content. One of our conclusions is that a strong emotional investment can result in encapsulation. The investment might be in a particular approach to biblical interpretation, or to particular religious concepts and experiences, or to secular ideas and experiences (e.g., a strongly negative view of authority and the function of law in our society).

Encapsulation is only one explanation for mixed perspectives within persons. Perhaps even more prevalent is the influence of certain contexts upon our ways of thinking about different subjects. For example, some engineers or politicians might use Conceptualizing Charles's analytical approach in their work, but then might think more like Affiliating Al with regard to their families, where their authority is unquestioned and family harmony is a top priority. Also, people who experience their local congregation as a "family" (in terms of interpersonal relationships; perspective A) may have great difficulty in conceptualizing its institutional dimensions (perspective C); yet they may understand and make appeals to the institutional character of their work and societal responsibilities. The emphasis on critical thinking (perspective C) that we find in the context of higher education is another example of an implicit standard that uses one perspective as normative. Such observations raise questions about how faith perspectives should be used. Do we want people to think consistently from a single perspective? Is consistency the best criterion for evaluating how a person makes his or her way in the world? Should we strive for more A than C, or more D than B? What perspective, if any, should be normative for determining the adequacy or maturity of being a Christian? And from what perspective does a response to these questions get formulated? We will consider these and other questions as we continue to explore how perspectives of faith can help us understand and work with one another.

7

TEACHING AND PERSPECTIVAL INTERPRETATIONS

This is a point of wisdom, I guess, that you can say you are wise when you have reached the point when you know there is so much more to learn, and I'm realizing how people have been studying [the Bible] for centuries and still keep finding something, and I just know there is a wealth of stuff here. — Betty4

"What do you think?" Jesus introduced parables with this question to engage the thinking of his learners (see Matt. 18:12; 21:28; Luke 10:36). He often left them wondering without providing them with the "right" answer. That is what parables do to people. That is also what people do. They wonder. They think. They invent meaning. They interpret.

Interpretation is the heart of teaching. Both student and instructor come to the subject matter from a particular horizon or point of view that affects how they will interact with that information. Their process of interpretation enables them to appropriate new information into their self-understandings and worldviews, where its impact makes a difference in their lives. Understanding takes place in the relationship between content or text and interpreter, and it transforms them both.[1] In addition to transmitting information about the Bible, teachers can help learners develop interpretive abilities, rather than providing them with normative interpretations. Dialogue with the Bible by both teacher and student can provide the opportunity for the Bible to exert a revelatory force in each interpreter's search for meaning. As one dimension of that meaning, self-understanding and knowledge of the Bible help learners locate themselves in their traditions and communities of interpretation.[2]

---

1. See Rudolf Bultmann, "The Problem of Hermeneutics," in *Essays: Philosophical and Theological* (New York: Macmillan, 1955), 234–61, for formulating the problem of interpretation in terms of how understanding can take place.

2. H. Edward Everding Jr., "A Hermeneutical Approach to Educational Theory," in *Foundations for Christian Education in an Era of Change*, ed. Marvin J. Taylor (Nashville: Abingdon, 1976), 41–53.

Perspectival Interpretations

Perspectives of faith shape how we interpret the Bible. In previous chapters, we have seen how four adult perspectives of faith result in very different responses to the authority and images of the Bible. Biblical texts are also interpreted quite differently by each perspective. How can the teacher and student gain greater understanding of this diversity and work with it creatively in teaching and learning situations?

Teachers can anticipate some of the diversity of interpretations of a biblical text by constructing perspectival interpretation grids. Such a grid provides one way to take the role of persons who interpret concepts out of different faith perspectives. It seeks to enhance understanding and communication between teacher and learner. A grid "not only raises relevant questions related to the students' probable grasp of material, but also opens up new vistas for the instructor. Accepted assumptions may be challenged, facilitating new awareness in role-taking."[3] We suggest the following steps for a teacher as preparation for a class.

- *Step 1:* Complete your own study of the content you plan to teach, for example, a text, topic, concept, or curriculum material.

- *Step 2:* Identify major concepts that emerge from the content.

- *Step 3:* Identify the age groups and perspectives you will be teaching. For example,
    Junior high: Perspectives A and B
    Senior high: Perspectives A, B, and C
    Adult: Perspectives A, B, C, and D

- *Step 4:* Look at the table of adult perspectives of faith (see table 2, chapter 1, pages 22–23). Select subject areas that might shed light on how each perspective will interpret the concepts that you have identified. List these subject areas in the left column of the grid, leaving spaces for the relevant perspectives.

- *Step 5:* Construct how one relevant perspective might interpret a particular concept. If you can, suggest differing interpretations for that perspective (e.g., pro and con) to distinguish the *structure* of thinking from the *content* expressed.

- *Step 6:* Continue with the other perspectives, and then repeat the process with the next concept(s).

---

3. The process of gridding was introduced by Wilcox, *Developmental Journey,* 217–21, 234–42. The quotation is from p. 220.

As an illustration, we'll construct a partial grid for the parable of the good Samaritan in Luke 10:30–35. Other examples will be introduced later in this chapter.

Step 1: Choice of content and study: the parable of the good Samaritan.

"A man was going down from Jerusalem to Jericho, and fell into the hands of robbers, who stripped him, beat him, and went away, leaving him half dead. Now by chance a priest was going down that road; and when he saw him, he passed by on the other side. So likewise a Levite, when he came to the place and saw him, passed by on the other side. But a Samaritan while traveling came near him; and when he saw him, he was moved with pity. He went to him and bandaged his wounds, having poured oil and wine on them. Then he put him on his own animal, brought him to an inn, and took care of him. The next day he took out two denarii, gave them to the innkeeper, and said, 'Take care of him; and when I come back, I will repay you whatever more you spend.'" (Luke 10:30–35 NRSV)

After studying the parable apart from its literary context in Luke, we have concluded that the story invites us to identify with the victim. Although he is anonymously introduced, we think this person is a Jew who is leaving Jerusalem for home in Jericho. As the victim, we would expect first the priest and then the Levite to come to our assistance, but they do not. The only option in the story for the victim's being saved is through a mortal enemy, the Samaritan, who would not be expected to give assistance. The reversal of expectations in the story has the capacity to subvert a worldview of insiders versus outsiders or of a hierarchy of priest, Levite, common Jew, enemy. "Utterly rejected is any notion that the kingdom can be marked off as religious: The map no longer has boundaries. The kingdom does not separate insiders and outsiders on the basis of religious categories."[4]

Step 2: Major concepts: Of the various concepts and images suggested by our study (e.g., the victim's plight, the actions of the Samaritan, being "moved with pity"), we have selected the victim's expectations or views of the priest, Levite, and Samaritan.

---

4. The quotation is from Bernard Brandon Scott, *Hear Then the Parable: A Commentary on the Parables of Jesus* (Minneapolis: Fortress, 1989), 201–2. The focus on the victim and the "imaginative shock" produced by the parable was earlier introduced by Robert W. Funk, *Language, Hermeneutic, and Word of God: The Problem of Language in the New Testament and Contemporary Theology* (New York: Harper & Row, 1966), 199ff. The reversal of expectations in the parable, its subverting effect, and its challenge to experience the inbreaking of the kingdom characterize the interpretation by John Dominic Crossan, *In Parables: The Challenge of the Historical Jesus* (New York: Harper & Row, 1973), 57–66.

Step 3: Participants' perspectives: a young adult class ranging in age from twenty-one to thirty-two and representing perspectives A, B, and C.

Step 4: Subject areas of faith perspectives appropriate to the concepts: Because we have chosen the victim's views of priest, Levite, and Samaritan, the following subject areas might be used.

- "Persons," because the victim views the characters in terms of their characteristics or values as persons

- "Value of human life," because the victim has expectations about how the characters will value his life

- "Role-taking," because the victim would try to take the role of the characters

We'll illustrate the process by using the subject area "Role-taking" in table 2 (chapter 1, pages 22–23). We'll complete the theory part of the grid as follows on table 7:

Table 7
Perspectival Interpretation Grid on Role-Taking
in the Parable of the Good Samaritan: Theory

Subject Area and Perspective	Concept: Victim's View of Priest and Levite	Concept: Victim's View of Samaritan
ROLE-TAKING: PERSPECTIVE A Projecting into feelings of others if not too different from oneself; empathy for the "unfortunate," if deserved		
ROLE-TAKING: PERSPECTIVE B Tolerance for letting people "do their own thing" as long as they do not impose on others. Understands nonabsolutist perspective, engages in some stereotyping		
ROLE-TAKING: PERSPECTIVE C Taking the role of others in context of similar social systems and values		

Step 5: Perspectival interpretations: How might the victim view the priest and the Levite? How might the victim view the Samaritan? See table 8 for examples.

Table 8
Perspectival Interpretation Grid on Role-Taking
in the Parable of the Good Samaritan: Complete

Subject Area and Perspective	Concept: Victim's View of Priest and Levite	Concept: Victim's View of Samaritan
ROLE-TAKING: PERSPECTIVE A Projecting into feelings of others if not too different from oneself; empathy for the "unfortunate," if deserved	Would expect them to help because of his needful situation; they ought to be sympathetic for him because he didn't deserve this treatment. They might not help him, if they feel he doesn't deserve their assistance.	Would not expect him to help, because he is an enemy of the Jews. He might help if he thinks the victim is also a Samaritan.
ROLE-TAKING: PERSPECTIVE B Tolerance for letting people "do their own thing" as long as they do not impose on others. Understands nonabsolutist perspective, engages in some stereotyping	Would expect them to help him if they feel like doing something. If they don't help him, it is because they feel they have more important things to do.	Would not expect him to help, because he feels that he might also get robbed or that he shouldn't get involved with a Jew. He might help, if he wants to.
ROLE-TAKING: PERSPECTIVE C Taking the role of others in context of similar social systems and values	Would expect them to help him because of their shared commitment to Judaism and their religious value of helping a fellow Jew. They might not help him, if they adjudge him to be dead, which would defile them.	Would not expect him to help, because Jews and Samaritans do not share common religious traditions, beliefs, and worship. He might help, if he can appeal to some common value that Jews and Samaritans share despite their religious and social differences.

Step 6: Next concept: Perhaps one could construct a grid for the Samaritan's being "moved with pity" or other actions of the Samaritan, etc.

Perspectival Teaching and Learning Processes

Information discovered through perspectival interpretation grids can be fruitful for many kinds of teaching and learning processes. The practice of gridding not only helps students and teachers see different dimensions of a biblical text; it is also a helpful way to keep in mind the specific needs of individual learners. In this section, we illustrate the use of the grid for three types of teaching and learning processes: instructional, relational, and transformational.

Instructional Process

Instructional processes focus on the presentation of information by the teacher. The format might be lectures, audiovisuals, discussions, discovery techniques, or experiential activities designed to facilitate students' understanding and assimilating of the information. This is the most common method used with almost all curriculum materials.

The following exercise is designed to help students interpret key concepts in Ephesians 4:1–16 and to work with students' different perspectives of faith. With the help of the instructor, students complete the following steps for developing a perspectival interpretation grid. To facilitate the process, the instructor predetermines the major concepts to be "love" and "the body of Christ."

Steps 1 and 2: Have the students complete the "interpretation tasks" in the handout, on page 77, "An Exercise in Biblical Interpretation."

Without suggesting that there are "right" answers to the first two interpretation questions, the instructor's answers can be shared with the students so that they can compare and contrast what they have discovered with what the instructor discovered. The following brief summaries are examples of how the first two questions might be answered.

> In Ephesians 4, love is a communal human quality characterized by individuals "bearing with one another" (4:2), speaking the truth with one another, and resulting in the building up of the body.

> In Ephesians 4, the body of Christ consists of individuals with special gifts, and the saints, whose responsibility is to build up the community toward maturity in Christ; each part works together to promote this bodily growth.

Step 3: Ask the students to teach a group of adults representing perspectives A, B, C, and D. They are to use Ephesians 4:1–16 and focus on the concepts "love" and "the body of Christ."

Step 4: Ask the students to select subject areas from the table of adult perspectives of faith (see table 2, chapter 1, pages 22–23) that can shed light on how each perspective will interpret the two concepts. The instructor may guide students' selections, suggesting the subject area "Role-taking" for love, because love relates to how persons perceive and treat other persons, and suggesting the subject area "Community/society" for the body of Christ, because the body pertains to a social organization.

Step 5: Ask the students to construct how the four perspectives might interpret the concepts "love" and "the body of Christ." The following examples, on pages 78 and 79, are in the form of handouts, which can serve as models for the students to follow or as examples to compare and contrast with their own constructions.

An Exercise in Biblical Interpretation

Text: Ephesians 4:1–16 (NRSV modified)

[1]I therefore, the prisoner in the Lord, beg you to lead a life worthy of the calling to which you have been called, [2]with all humility and gentleness, with patience, bearing with one another in love, [3]making every effort to maintain the unity of the Spirit in the bond of peace. [4]There is one body and one Spirit, just as you were called to the one hope of your calling, [5]one Lord, one faith, one baptism, [6]one God and Father of all, who is above all and through all and in all.

[7]But each of us was given grace according to the measure of Christ's gift. [8]Therefore it is said,

> "When he ascended on high he made captivity itself a captive;
> he gave gifts to his people."

[9]When it says, *"He ascended,"* what does it mean but that he had also descended into the lower parts of the earth? [10]He who descended is the same one who ascended far above all the heavens, so that he might fill all things. [11]The *gifts he gave* were that some would be apostles, some prophets, some evangelists, some pastors and teachers, [12]to equip the saints for the work of ministry, for building up the body of Christ, [13]until all of us come to the unity of the faith and of the knowledge of the Son of God, to maturity, to the measure of the full stature of Christ. [14]We must no longer be children, tossed to and fro and blown about by every wind of doctrine, by people's trickery, by their craftiness in deceitful scheming. [15]But speaking the truth in love, we must grow up in every way into him who is the head, into Christ, [16]from whom the whole body, joined and knit together by every ligament with which it is equipped, as each part is working properly, promotes the body's growth in building itself up in love.

Interpretation Tasks

1. What does the text say about
   a. love
   b. the body of Christ?

2. What did the text mean about
   a. love
   b. the body of Christ?

3. What does the text mean for your understanding of
   a. love
   b. the body of Christ?

Perspectival Interpretations

Ephesians 4:1–16 (NRSV)

I... beg you to lead a life worthy of the calling to which you have been called,... bearing with one another in *love*.... There is one *body*... one faith.... But each of us was given grace ... to equip the saints for the work of ministry, for building up the *body* of Christ, until all of us come to the unity of the faith.... Speaking the truth in *love,* we must grow up in every way into him who is the head, into Christ, from whom the whole *body,* joined and knit together by every ligament with which it is equipped, as each part is working properly, promotes the *body's* growth in building itself up in *love.*

Perspectival Interpretations of Love

Perspective A: Love is seen in terms of a focus on interpersonal relationships based in feelings: "How can I love someone I don't like?" There is stereotyping and rejection of those I don't like. Interpersonal ties are enduring and not to be disrupted. Example:

> The author calls this group to bind itself together in love. If persons do not exhibit virtues such as humility, gentleness, patience, and bearing with one another, then they don't belong among the saints. Everyone should be concerned with strengthening the group and its values.

Perspective B: Love is seen in terms of interpersonal relationships based in feelings: "I'll love someone if I feel like it." Love might mean something different to someone else; it depends on how that person feels about it. Example:

> The author calls this group to bind itself together in love, but that doesn't mean that the saints have to think or act alike, or even like each other all the time. The text states that "each of us was given grace," which means that we are different. Maybe unity here means that we can agree to disagree, but it doesn't mean we have to be uniform.

Perspective C: Love can be abstract, moving beyond the interpersonal; we can love those we neither know nor like, if their value systems are similar to ours. We can love the sinner but dislike the sin. Example:

> In this text, "love" refers to the energy or life force that both enlivens and causes growth of the body. "Love" is a structuring power that enables persons to support one another and speak the truth to one another regardless of their personal feelings about one another.

Perspective D: To love means to value all persons equally. It does not depend on good feelings or on value systems. Each person has intrinsic value. Example:

> In this text, "love" refers to one's capacity to value all persons as of equal worth. To bear with one another and speak the truth with one another are ways that persons embody their commitment to the intrinsic value of each individual regardless of any limiting criteria such as gender, role, status, or position of importance within the community.

Perspectival Interpretations of the Body of Christ

Perspective A: The body of Christ, the church, is composed of interpersonal relationships; its unity is maintained through prevention of dissension. There is stereotyping of those who don't "fit" or are disruptive, and they are excluded. Example:

> Clearly, the body of Christ, for this author, is composed of only those who adhere to the one truth and love each other. Persons who don't believe the faith and don't love others in the group simply do not belong. The author excludes those who teach false doctrine and who scheme to deceive people.

Perspective B: The body of Christ is composed of everyone who feels that they want to belong to the believing community. "If they don't feel that way about it, then they might want to belong to another community or none at all. That is their opinion, and who am I to say it's not true? I'd even welcome them into our group, even if they didn't feel they wanted to belong." Example:

> I wonder who the author is angry about? Maybe those who trick and scheme just don't conform to the author's idea of one faith and one body. The author's emphasis on the one body that is based on the saints' uniform belief and on loving those who share that belief makes me a bit uncomfortable. I want more room to disagree and to express my own feelings.

Perspective C: The body of Christ is a structured system whose major purpose is to maintain its value systems as expressed through laws, doctrines, traditions, rituals, symbols, and so forth. Example:

> This text uses the term *body* to refer to the church as an institution composed of gifted individuals or officials (4:11) and saints (4:12), who together contribute to the maintenance and growth of the church.

Perspective D: The body of Christ is an interdependent community composed of diverse and growing persons who derive their vision from Christ. Acceptance of all persons makes it possible to speak the truth in love for each person and for the whole body. If one falters, the whole body suffers. Example:

> Although the word *body* probably refers to the church as an institution concerned about its identity, maintenance, and growth, the process by which this takes place involves the interdependence of those with special gifts, the saints, and the author (who embodies a form of relinquishment leadership by identifying with the process of the body's growth in 4:13, that is, "all of us"). As a transcendent vision, "the full stature of Christ" is a lure for this growth process of love, unity, and knowledge.

Relational Process

Relational teaching and learning processes include both individual (e.g., prayer, meditation) and group activities, projects, and experiences. Relational approaches emphasize the unique synergy of a communal context for growth in self-understanding and commitment. The diversity that perspectives of faith represent becomes quickly apparent in a communal approach to biblical interpretation. Teachers can interpret the plurality of perspectives in a learning context as a richness that can benefit each student's self-understanding. In a supportive environment that encourages self-expression and the exchange of ideas, exposure to different perspectives and interpretations can be a very effective means of broadening and deepening the faith of the participants. Teachers can affirm and facilitate such a process by developing a context of trust, including interacting with different ways of interpreting a text, role-taking different perspectives, and presenting options for persons' perspectives by suggesting alternative interpretations.

The following group Bible study engages learners in interpreting Matthew 12:9–14 and in using their imaginations to take different faith perspectives. Each small group can brainstorm how all four faith perspectives might interpret the concepts, or each could deal with just one of the perspectives. In the latter case, communal interpretations can be enhanced by having the small groups role-play the faith perspectives they represent in a debate or simulated community discussion.

A Bible Study

Text: Matthew 12:9–14 (NRSV modified)

[9]Jesus left that place and entered their synagogue; [10]a man was there with a withered hand, and the Pharisees asked him, "Is it lawful to cure on the sabbath?" so that they might accuse him. [11]He said to them, "Suppose one of you has only one sheep and it falls into a pit on the sabbath; will you not lay hold of it and lift it out? [12]How much more valuable is a human being than a sheep! So it is lawful to do good on the sabbath." [13]Then he said to the man, "Stretch out your hand." He stretched it out, and it was restored, as sound as the other. [14]But the Pharisees went out and conspired against him, how to destroy him.

Interpretation Tasks

1. Read and study the story.
2. Suggest how each perspective of faith might interpret the following:
   a. the Pharisees
   b. Jesus' breaking of the Law
   c. "How much more valuable is a human being than a sheep!"
   d. the true meaning of the story

Suggestions for how each perspective might interpret the concepts, as on the following handout, "Perspectival Interpretations of Matthew 12:9– 14," could be distributed for learners to compare their interpretations.[5] These perspectival interpretations were developed based on the following: (*a*) the subject area "Persons" for the Pharisees; (*b*) the subject area "Law" for Jesus' breaking of the law; (*c*) the subject area "Value of human life" for "How much more valuable is a human being than a sheep!" and (*d*) the subject area "Truth" for the true meaning of the story.

Perspectival Interpretations of Matthew 12:9–14

Perspective A

a. *The Pharisees:* The Pharisees were trying to prevent chaos, but they were still bad guys because they were trying to kill Jesus and didn't seem to care that a person's life is precious.

b. *Jesus' breaking of the Law:* "Laws should only be made so they let people grow more fully, so Jesus should have broken the law, because he was totally giving. Yeah, because he was helping somebody."

c. *"How much more valuable is a human being than a sheep!"* "Neither one, because we're all valuable; everything is interrelated. I think they're both the same, important, they're both helpful. I put more value on human life, like it's absolutely taboo to take another person's life. I guess I have more empathy for humans."

d. *The true meaning of the story.* Well, Jesus gives us an example of helping those in need. He embodies God's love for all persons in need of healing, sustenance, and protection.

Perspective B

a. *The Pharisees:* The Pharisees wanted to accuse Jesus of disobeying the law to show that if others followed his example, then people would just be looking out for themselves.

b. *Jesus' breaking of the Law:* Jesus should have broken the law, because he felt that's what he wanted to do, and felt that the Pharisees should know better than to impose a bad law in this situation.

c. *"How much more valuable is a human being than a sheep!"* A person's life is more important than greed, money, drugs, or even obeying the law.

d. *The true meaning of the story.* I can only say what it means for me, but it probably means something different for everyone who reads it. What works for me is to read it as a teaching about the importance of helping others in need, even when that might go against a law, such as a curfew or a stoplight.

---

5. Some of the suggestions represent our constructions of hypothetical responses based on information about the perspectives, much as the gridding process is designed to do. Others (appearing in quotation marks) are based on quotations from our early research project, reported in Everding and Wilcox, "Implications of Kohlberg's Theory."

Perspectival Interpretations of Matthew 12:9–14

Perspective C

a. *The Pharisees:* The Pharisees accused Jesus of disobeying the law because he posed a very definite threat to the stability of their society.

b. *Jesus' breaking of the Law:* Jesus should have broken the law, but the question might be raised, could not Jesus have waited until Monday? The basic point then becomes not the healing of the person but the establishment for the Pharisees of the fact that there was something drastically wrong with their interpretation of the law and with their understanding of the law's relationship to life.

c. *"How much more valuable is a human being than a sheep!"* All life, human or otherwise, is sacred. Yet I think a person is more important than an animal, because humans are capable of emotion and several other processes. Humans are more complex. Animals are not conscious. They don't think and they're not in control.

d. *The true meaning of the story.* The question for the Matthean community — and the pastoral problem that Matthew had to address — was the manner in which the Sabbath was to be observed. The principles derived from Matthew 12:9–14 are compassion toward others and doing good. This second principle may also allude to the summary of the Torah as loving God and neighbor.

Perspective D

a. *The Pharisees:* I understand that the Pharisees accused Jesus of disobeying the law because he posed a very definite threat to the stability of their society, but laws should be designed for the protection of universal human rights. In this case, I think they applied the Sabbath law in too literal a way so that it became unreasonable as far as its intent to promote "rest" and wholeness.

b. *Jesus' breaking of the Law:* It's a question of how the law is to be interpreted. Jesus was not intending to do away with the law. It bothers me in terms of the effect it's going to have on the Pharisees if they see the law as keeping their whole religious system from falling apart. Maybe Jesus was trying to change the law to allow them to treat people with mercy.

c. *"How much more valuable is a human being than a sheep!"* Human life is more important than animal life. As far as we know, humans are the only kind of creature who finds and attributes meaning to all the rest of the universe, who can make what we call moral decisions and take ethical responsibility.

d. *The true meaning of the story.* Well, for today this story challenges me to examine my core values. I am aware that societies and institutions require rules and regulations to maintain their systems, but when those rules and regulations become contaminated with biases that exclude persons because of their appearance, disability, age, or sexual orientation, then I think it's time to change the rules and regulations. The story causes me to reflect on the possible contamination of my own commitments and the commitments of my community of faith.

Transformational Process

Transformational teaching and learning processes involve creating a safe environment in which a person can be challenged to see the world and his or her faith experience with new eyes. Issues that deal with authority, truth, and role-taking frequently provide opportunities for persons to encounter different perspectives in very powerful ways.[6] Learning to explain their own perspective and/or "trying on" other perspectives involves persons in testing the boundaries of diversity. Often, just having the option of considering different perspectives of faith stimulates transformation. Based on our research, we have come to the conclusion that transformations within perspectives or from one perspective to another involve a long-term process and are not automatic. Experiences that plant the seeds of change or nurture tentative new growth are an important part of that process.

The rank order on page 84 about the authority of God and the Bible provides an initial opportunity to think about how one values the Bible and thinks about authority. Ask learners to rank order the five statements as indicated in the instructions. After all have completed that task, have them report their rank orders, and record them on a chalkboard or on newsprint. Give persons the opportunity to explain why they ordered the statements the way they did, but instruct them that there is to be no debate or critique of opinions expressed. After the period of sharing, ask learners whether they would change their ranking, and if so, why.

Following the rank order exercise or in a subsequent session, introduce the different ways that perspectives of faith understand the authority of the Bible. The handout on pages 85 and 86, drawing upon quotations from the Biblical Interviews, can be used with various techniques. All may read it and share which views they prefer or dislike. Small groups can discuss all four perspectives or just one perspective, which they might then role-play in a debate or discussion. All might discuss the strengths and weaknesses of each perspective's view, and so on.

---

6. Perhaps the most powerful examples of transformational processes are so-called immersion experiences, in which persons literally place themselves in the context of another culture (e.g., youth mission trips), a different social class (e.g., living and working with inner-city kids), or an extreme life situation (e.g., Outward Bound programs). For effective transformation, the "immersion experience" should be followed by in-depth reflection and analysis.

Rank Order: The Authority of God and the Bible

Read the following descriptions of God and the Bible. Then rank them in order from the one with which you most strongly agree (number 1) to the one with which you most strongly disagree (number 5). If you do not agree with any, add your own description and rank all six.

A. _____ God is all-powerful and unchanging, and so the message of the Bible does not change. The Spirit gives us the faith to accept and believe that message.

B. _____ God has given us the Bible as a blueprint for living, the only record we have of the example Christ gave us for living our lives. The Bible is a guidebook, a direct source of discovering what God requires of us. It is the standard by which we discern the Spirit in our own lives.

C. _____ The Bible is the story of how the people of God responded to particular situations. Through a historical understanding of the Bible, we can learn how we might respond today.

D. _____ The essence of God is unchanging, but God's purposive action is always changing, responding to the world's situation and then influencing according to God's eternal purpose. The Bible is the gift to us that helps us engage in this process.

E. _____ The Bible in all its complexity can be experienced almost as another person with whom we can dialogue, whom we interpret and who interprets us, within the ongoing presence of God/Christ/Spirit.

F. _____ (Your own description)

Faith Perspectives on the Authority of the Bible

Perspective A:

The authority of the Bible is interpreted as external and absolute. It provides normative guidelines or rules or doctrines that are sanctioned by the group with which one is affiliated. Its authority may be described in terms of inerrancy, a canon within the canon, *sola scriptura,* or other standard. Reasoning about authority may be tacit and stereotypical. Examples:

1. "[The scriptures] have authority because God said they have authority!"

2. "I guess I would say that the authority I give to the scripture is basically presenting the values, accepting the values presented in the scriptures, and I don't know if I can give any reason why for one value being better than another."

3. "Absolute standards come from an absolute authority, God. And that absolute authority has given us the truth in the Bible."

Perspective B:

The authority of the Bible is interpreted in terms of one's personal feelings or preferences. Its authority is still external and absolute, but persons can relate to it in any way that is meaningful for them. Examples:

1. "I guess I'll just have to say the authority comes from the inspiration of God to people who care about wanting to impart faith to others, and what they have gained from it.... God is the ultimate authority."

2. "I have been in places where it has been absolutely impossible for me to get across my understanding of how the Bible is an authority for me. But the Bible is an authority for other people in a different understanding."

3. "I would affirm that the scripture is the word of God, but not always.... And I would state very clearly that this is my opinion only and is not absolute and is not the final word."

Faith Perspectives on the Authority of the Bible

Perspective C:

The authority of the Bible is located internally through the interpreter's logically determined truth or the internalized authority of the biblical writers. The Bible's authority may also be located in a system, for example, as prescribed by one's church or denomination according to the criteria used in that institution's process of selection and ratification of scriptures. Examples:

1. "My argument for the authority of the scripture would have to be its utility in my own life and in other persons' lives, as opposed to some other granting them authority by the church or by an authority or by God."

2. "Some of the reasons that I might give to someone for the authority of the scriptures would be their validity for all times. I mean, they have...lasted for years and years, decades, generations, in all kinds of situations,...that they speak, are universally translatable."

3. "I would accept the authority of the church and the tradition of the church as the authority of the scripture."

Perspective D:

The authority of the Bible is partial, in that it relates to other authorities (e.g., tradition, reason, and experience) that are weighed in a dialectical process. The result is internalized in personal and contextualized commitment rooted in examined experience in history and community. It is also ultimate, in that it is a bearer of the reality to which it refers and it evokes participation in and commitment to that reality on the part of its hearers/readers whose lives are invaded by it. Examples:

1. "It's really the expression of the humanity of people who have lived, and because of that there's real authority in that as an expression of humanity, an expression of what life has meant to some people."

2. "The authority of the scripture comes out of an authoritative vision and intention on the part of all the writers of the scripture, who [were] inspired by their understanding, their experience, their rational beliefs about and their vision of what it means to be engaged in an active life of faith in relationship with God within a community, a particular community of faith. The intention is to say something about the relationship of persons to God and to one another in the search for meaning and understanding of life's experiences and questions."

3. "The Bible has authority because of the people in the Bible, in all those stories, in all those situations; I would give authority because they had authority.... Also, I give authority because it has been authority in terms of tradition and the tradition of the Bible, going back into oral tradition of the Bible, prior to that time the Hebrews wrote it; those spoken words even had authority."

Perspectives on Teaching and Learning

The variables involved in the teaching and learning process multiply when we begin to consider the implications of interacting perspectives of faith. For example, what are the implications for a teacher whose faith perspective is predominantly that of Conceptualizing Charles but whose learners are predominantly Affiliating Als and Bargaining Bettys? Or what would be the outcome if a teacher's faith perspective is mostly Al's but the learners are mostly Charleses? The way content (information, ideas) is presented should be appropriate for the learners' faith perspective. That is, content should be both accessible and challenging. However, coordinating the perspectives of adult learners and teachers could prove to be a difficult, if not impossible, task. Examining the typical perceptions of teachers and learners from each of the four adult perspectives provides a means for evaluating what happens in an educational situation. It may also help teachers think about their own faith perspective and about ways they might enrich it toward the goal of treating learners as interpreting subjects with inherent value, not passive recipients.[7]

Perspective A: Affiliating Al

AS TEACHER

As a teacher, Al views himself as the authority who shepherds what the learners do and say. He is the expert; they are the novices. The position of having the truth gives Al self-confidence in what he teaches, so he is able to communicate with clarity and forcefulness. He sees learners as seekers of the knowledge he can impart, but not as active thinkers and evaluators.

AS LEARNER

As a learner, Al considers the teacher to be the authority in the classroom. The teacher tells Al what to do and has the right answers. This means that information taught in the course is true and correct, and that there are only right and wrong answers. Learning is hearing without evaluation and being able to give back the right answers. Al tends to view himself as a passive recipient of knowledge and is dependent on the teacher for learning the right answers. He thinks class discussions are a waste of time, because other students do not have the correct information. He also resists logic and analysis, considering them irrelevant. Although feeling like an empty vessel to be filled, Al has a strong sense of fairness in how that is accomplished by the teacher.

---

7. The following descriptions are constructions based on each faith perspective's way of thinking about the subject areas "Authority," "Truth," and "Role-taking."

IMPLICATIONS

Al's way of thinking about authority and truth offers stability, security, and comfort. For Al, there is absolute truth and there are authorities or experts and scripture to teach the truth. However, truth and authority can be appropriated in different ways, depending on the *content* of what the authority deems to be true. Another important factor is the extent to which deep feelings are attached to the particular content of truth. That is, persons using perspective A can be closed-thinking or open-thinking, loving and accepting in some areas and unloving and judgmental in others. The point is that ways of thinking absolutely about truth and authority may be mixed with reasoning skills that tend to compartmentalize and stereotype. Nevertheless, Al's perspective of faith provides rich opportunities for interpretation by generating ideas and hypotheses about the meaning of biblical texts. This style of thinking, moreover, lends itself to transformation because of its potential for broadening and deepening persons' ability both to think solemnly and to feel strongly about what they believe. The inability to separate thinking from feeling, however, may be a limiting factor to interpretation, unless Al encounters complex ideas, issues, and concerns that can entice him to consider the need for different forms or patterns of thinking. Experiences with trusted and respected persons who think differently from Al can also contribute to transformation within his perspective.

Perspective B: Bargaining Betty

AS TEACHER

Betty may feel a loss of authority as a teacher, without understanding exactly why. She may have difficulty in justifying her own opinions, because she is unclear about (and unable to benefit from) the use of rational criteria. With the realization that there is no absolute truth, she may feel insecure or threatened. Alternatively, she might feel a new sense of freedom in not being tied to material that she would like to question on the basis of her feelings and preferences. Betty gives credibility to students' opinions but may not be able to justify her own opinions in debate with students who use analysis and rationality.

AS LEARNER

As a learner, Betty suspects that the teacher's opinions are no better than her own and that she does not need to accept what the teacher says. This creates a new feeling of autonomy and self-directedness. Betty values her own opinion and tolerates the right of others to have their own opinions. However, she may feel a loss of confidence in what she believes when she is unable to justify her own opinions through objective criteria. Moreover, she distrusts logic and analysis or may feel threatened by them. Betty may enjoy discussions based on opinions rather than logic. On the other hand, she may be excited by the possibilities that analytic thinking suggests to her.

IMPLICATIONS

The tacit and nonanalytical (or quasi-analytical) features of perspective B constitute a possible downside for Betty. How far can tolerance be stretched when it is based on the sole criterion of "what anyone feels is right"? Bargaining Betty really has no reasonable way to adjudicate among truth claims. If she is bombarded with too much multiplicity, she may withdraw because of turmoil and frustration. When she finds herself in an environment where critical thinking is the norm (e.g., college), she is often labeled "individualist," "relativist," "a fuzzy thinker," or "incoherent and inconsistent." Unfortunately, those kinds of labels can have the effect of shutting down her characteristic openness to discovering new things and different interpretations.

Betty's multiplistic perspective of faith provides one way of creating and sustaining community based on the common ground of how each person "feels" about a subject. If persons permit each other with friendship and tolerance to share their feelings and thoughts about what they hold to be true, then they may have the opportunity to broaden and deepen their own understandings. Depending on the ground rules for this kind of exchange, perspective B thinkers may grow in their ability to listen and empathize with other ways of thinking. They will not, however, be able by themselves to create a just community based on critical reflection, understanding, and acceptance.

Many perspective B thinkers display self-perceptions as interpreters who are open, excited, and eager about learning and changing. How important it is in congregations to respond to that openness with equal enthusiasm about their growth! What a challenge and opportunity Betty$_4$ presents for educators and pastors when she says,

> I wonder about the Bible in the context of the civilization that was going on, the writing that was going on, all the changing qualities of civilization which would be able to have an effect on it.... Any doubts that I would have would be offset by the fact that I believe it to be the inspiration of God, that there is a message that can come through from the story of the creation that, while I don't take it literally, I wonder about it.... This is a point of wisdom, I guess, that you can say you are wise when you have reached the point when you know there is so much more to learn, and I'm realizing how people have been studying this for centuries and still keep finding something, and I just know there is a wealth of stuff here.

Perspective C: Conceptualizing Charles

AS TEACHER

As a teacher, Charles tends to place confidence in the credentialing institution and its values and therefore in his own role as representative of that institution. Charles values highly a focus on critical thinking skills. If sensitive to the learners, Charles will view them as persons who need to question, who need to debate and hear logical arguments, who can be encouraged to think for themselves in analytical ways. He has a tendency to focus on logical thinking and to devalue feelings, a tendency that may manifest itself in a bias against learners who rely on feelings.

AS LEARNER

As a learner, Charles develops skill in evaluating the teacher according to his expectations of the institution and, to some extent, according to his internalized values. Charles will have respect for a teacher who has appropriate credentials and who lives up to them according to Charles's standards. He favors the teacher who explains content using logic and analysis but may reject the teacher who is absolutist or unable to defend his or her statements with rational criteria. Such a teacher will quickly lose credibility with Charles. Charles needs to feel in control of his learning process, to evaluate knowledge objectively, to be able to doubt, and to apply logic, especially to ideas based on feelings.

IMPLICATIONS

Charles feels most comfortable in settings that value critical thinking. The challenges for Charles as teacher or learner are to be open to and appreciative of different ways of thinking and to develop skills to communicate concepts, values, and his methods of analysis to persons who do not share his rational approach. Biblical content that emphasizes God's love for the other (e.g., the sinner, the outcast, the oppressed) invites Conceptualizing Charles to deepen his understanding and respect for persons who think differently from him.

Sometimes persons view Conceptualizing Charles as cold, aloof, unsympathetic, or calculating. (Perhaps he is bent on destroying "our" biblical beliefs by "picking them apart.") Sometimes persons see Charles as the type of intelligent and informed lay theologian that all persons might emulate, despite misgivings based on how he might seem (critical, arrogant, etc.). Perspective C rational thinkers are important assets for the faith community, because they can provide a way of creating and sustaining community based on the common ground of conceptual structures and organization. They develop laws, creeds, sanctions, and procedures that maintain institutions and their values. Thinkers like Charles can also be challenged to identify institutional values that can circumvent the tendency of systems to exclude and stereotype conflicting value systems. Can an institution such as the church be structured to embody the value of openness to all persons? Here again, it is *content* rather than *structure* that will determine what institutional values can protect the rights and feelings of persons who represent, for example, faith perspectives A and B. In his search for rationality, Charles can help the institution assess and incorporate alternative values that will enrich and extend the mission that Paul describes, which is to be the body of Christ in the world: "But speaking the truth in love, we must grow up in every way into him who is the head, into Christ, from whom the whole body, joined and knit together by every ligament with which it is equipped, as each part is working properly, promotes the body's growth in building itself up in love" (Eph. 4:15–16).

Perspective D: Dialectical Donna

AS TEACHER

Donna prefers to function as a resource for students as they plan, implement, and evaluate their own learning processes. At the same time, she understands something of the strengths and weaknesses of learners and the diversity of their perspectives, so she attempts to meet their individual needs. She may overwhelm her students with a variety of options and positions, but she can also provide strategies to examine and assess students. Most importantly, Donna considers herself a participant in the shared teaching and learning process, encouraging those learners whose approach is similar, while able to understand those whose approaches are different.

AS LEARNER

As a learner, Donna needs to hear a variety of views and to be presented with tools for evaluating them. She sees herself as engaged in an ongoing process of searching out new truths and reevaluating her commitments. Donna is able to empathize with the teacher and so is more tolerant of any limitations she might observe. She prefers to construct her own understanding of the course content and, even when a position of commitment is reached, tends to want to explore new understandings. Donna is in the process of reorganizing and integrating past insights into new paradigms. For her, paradox is a positive challenge. Alternatively, she may feel unheard and isolated in a group in which no one shares her perspective.

IMPLICATIONS

Persons using faith perspective D can be a valuable asset to the church and other institutions. They endorse methods and content for helping persons to develop critical thinking. They enjoy digging in and working on tough issues and concepts. Yet they cannot be totally satisfied with a search for rationality or didactic instructional models designed primarily to transmit information. Dialectical Donna is concerned to discover new ideas and meanings that she can integrate into her own conceptual framework and to which she can commit with both mind and heart. She seeks connections among various disciplines. She embraces rigorous academic approaches to various contents but desires to relate them to her own personal growth and professional development. She asks, "So what?" and pushes for a response that integrates analysis, affect, and commitment. Persons representing faith perspective D may find life lonely in the church. They have the capacity to "think like" the system but also to "stand outside" the system to evaluate and critique it. They seek to implement values such as openness; the equal worth of all types of thinking, feeling, and imagination; and relational ways of understanding truth. These are often unwelcome in institutional settings where the system's self-perpetuation requires uniform beliefs and commitments.

Dialectical Donna offers a shaping vision for creating and sustaining community based on the common ground of interest in, respect for, and understanding of persons as subjects and not objects. Her integrative way of thinking understands and values absolute and rational ways of thinking, even though she wants to incorporate them into new syntheses. Perspective D honors the personal and the objective, the interpersonal and the institutional, the cognitive and the affective. The existence of these different and often conflicting values challenges thinkers like Donna to translate understanding into forms of institutional life in which persons can not only coexist but also work together to promote "the body's growth in building itself up in love."

Perspectives on Curriculum

Concern for different perspectives of faith can enrich the development of curriculum for Christian nurture. In creating new curriculum, we advocate the inclusion of guidance for the teacher about how persons learn, self-reflection about the teacher's own perspective, the selection of appropriate materials, the positive function of diversity in the communal context, and compendiums of techniques and strategies, such as effective discussion questions.[8] Too often, the development and revision of curriculum focus excessively on the subject matter to be taught, the disciplines covered, the content territories protected, and so forth. Attending to perspectives of faith supports a learner-centered curriculum and provides a frame of reference for constructing and evaluating it.

---

8. For examples of effective questions, see Walter Wink, *Transforming Bible Study: A Leader's Guide* (Nashville: Abingdon, 1980); and Wayne Bradley Robinson, *The Transforming Power of the Bible* (New York: Pilgrim, 1984).

Part 2

Faith Perspectives and Christian Nurture

N OW THAT WE HAVE LOOKED in greater depth at four adult perspectives of faith as they are expressed in biblical interpretation, we will consider how the perspectives interact with some other content areas of Christian faith and life. In chapters 8 through 12, we explore how the perspectives impact our understanding and expression of five contents of religious life: belief, church, justice, empathy, and worship. We also suggest ways to nurture faith as a dynamic process in each of these areas.

Because nurture is understood to support and facilitate the inward process of broadening and deepening our experience and understanding of God, it should not be reduced to pushing or pulling persons to "higher" or different stages of faith. Christian nurture involves honoring the integrity of persons' ways of composing meaning from their experiences, supporting and challenging them to examine the adequacy of their perspectives, and providing opportunities for them to expand and enrich their understandings within the community of faith. Chapter 13 concludes by placing divergent perspectives of faith within the larger contemporary context that struggles to interpret and mediate diversity in daily life.

8

NURTURING FAITH PERSPECTIVES ON BELIEF

May the God of hope fill you with all joy and peace in believing, so that you may abound in hope by the power of the Holy Spirit.
— Romans 15:13 NRSV

Diversity of belief has characterized Christianity from its origins in the Jesus movement and the post-Easter understandings of Jesus as the risen Christ. A discussion in Mark's Gospel between Jesus and his disciples exemplifies that diversity. In response to Jesus' question "Who do people say that I am?" (Mark 8:27), the disciples report three possible alternatives (8:28). Even Peter's "correct" belief, that "You are the Messiah," is not correctly understood by Peter and results in Jesus' reprimand and explanation (8:31–34). We see another divergence of belief when Paul expounds his understanding of Jesus Christ as the one crucified, in opposition to Corinthians who believed that Jesus was the "wisdom of God" (1 Cor. 1 and 2).[1]

Contemporary Christians encounter diversity of Christian beliefs almost daily in church and society. Is God better understood as Father, Mother, or Parent? What are the differences between Protestant, Catholic, and Orthodox Christian beliefs? Why do some believe the Bible literally and others believe that the Bible is more appropriately read metaphorically? What are the differences between conservative and liberal Christians, between mainline and evangelical Christians? Diversity of belief is a common occurrence within our communities of faith.

---

1. Also representative of Christian diversity are two authors who write *about* diversity: Jaroslav Pelikan, *Jesus through the Centuries: His Place in the History of Culture* (New Haven, Conn.: Yale University Press, 1985); and James D. G. Dunn, *Unity and Diversity in the New Testament: An Inquiry into the Character of Earliest Christianity,* 2d ed. (Philadelphia: Trinity, 1990).

Faith Perspectives on the Bible and Its Interpretation

Numerous factors contribute to the diversity of Christian belief, for example, about the Bible and its interpretation. First, the Bible itself contains diverse strands of traditions and interpretations, such as the four portraits of Jesus in the Gospels or the various literary sources in the Pentateuch. The canonization of traditions such as these does not nullify their diversity. On the contrary, the canon as "standard" must be interpreted afresh for different times and places, illustrating a second source of diversity in biblical interpretation. A third factor resulting in differences in beliefs about the Bible is the variety of cultural contexts within which it is applied. For example, in their classic analysis of middle-class American cultural tendencies, Robert Bellah and his associates suggest that churches tend more to mirror American cultural understandings of expressive and utilitarian individualism than to serve as countercultural communities of public biblical justice.[2] Individualism in the culture, then, endorses and encourages an individualistic interpretation of the Bible.[3] Theological ideologies, social locations, and new methodologies also contribute to diversity in contemporary ways of thinking about the Bible and its meaning.[4]

Persons' perspectives of faith, as they demonstrate cognitive structures or locations, also contribute to the diversity of belief about the Bible and how it is understood. Earlier chapters have shown how perspectival interpretations of the images, tradition, and authority of the Bible can vary dramatically. If we consider a particular statement, such as "I believe in the Bible as the word of God," that belief may be understood and expressed differently by each perspective, as table 9 illustrates.

Perspectives of faith shape the way we understand and communicate our beliefs. They do not necessarily determine what beliefs persons hold. Each perspective, however, provides for those held beliefs an interpretive frame

---

2. Robert Bellah et al., *Habits of the Heart: Individualism and Commitment in American Life* (Berkeley: University of California Press, 1985), 219–49. For a similar distinction in two contemporary interpretations of youth ministry, see William Meyers, *Black and White Styles of Youth Ministry* (New York: Pilgrim, 1991).

3. For an interesting discussion of some of the diversity in biblical interpretation, see Nathan O. Hatch and Mark A. Noll, eds., *The Bible in America: Essays in Cultural History* (New York: Oxford University Press, 1982).

4. Contributions representing a plethora of contemporary views of the Bible and biblical interpretation include Letty M. Russell, ed., *Feminist Interpretation of the Bible* (Philadelphia: Westminster, 1985); Christopher Rowland and Mark Corner, *Liberating Exegesis: The Challenge of Liberation Theology to Biblical Studies* (Louisville, Ky.: Westminster/John Knox, 1989); R. S. Sugirtharajah, ed., *Voices from the Margin: Interpreting the Bible in the Third World* (Maryknoll, N.Y.: Orbis, 1991); Cain Hope Felder, ed., *Stony the Road We Trod: African American Biblical Interpretation* (Minneapolis: Fortress, 1991); Louise Schottroff, *Let the Oppressed Go Free: Feminist Perspectives on the New Testament* (Louisville, Ky.: Westminster/John Knox, 1991); Janice Capel Anderson and Stephen D. Moore, eds., *Mark and Method: New Approaches in Biblical Studies* (Minneapolis: Fortress, 1992); and Benton White, *Taking the Bible Seriously: Honest Differences about Biblical Interpretation* (Louisville, Ky.: Westminster/John Knox, 1993).

Table 9
Perspectival Interpretations of Belief about the Bible

The Bible as the word of God is understood as ...	
Perspective A ... God's absolute guidelines and truth, so I will seek the true meaning God reveals.	**Perspective C** ... the witness of persons' confrontation with God within the context of their communities and traditions, so I will struggle with the meanings of those witnesses and analyze them for their rational consistency.
Perspective B ... the way God speaks meaningfully to different persons, so I will seek the messages and guidelines that are useful for me.	**Perspective D** ... a subject that addresses me in such a way that I can be personally confronted by God within the context of community, so I find new ways of understanding my commitments by integrating fresh meanings I discover in dialogue with the Bible and with others.

of reference that, to the believer, constitutes "the way it is" (or ought to be). Each perspective has the capacity for both enlarging and constricting its vision of held beliefs. How, then, can we nurture perspectives on beliefs in a context that appreciates diversity and facilitates mutual understanding? This is the challenge for those concerned about Christian nurture.

Exploring Symbols of Beliefs

The following activities for a course or workshop provide opportunities for persons to explore faith perspectives on beliefs by focusing on their understanding of symbols. Participants usually find the opening exercise of choosing a symbol to be extremely meaningful, and it often evokes very deep and personal feelings. Care should be taken to honor these feelings, whether or not they are shared with the group. This activity establishes a context for exploring how each perspective of faith interprets symbol in general and religious symbols in particular.

Experiencing Symbols

The environment should enable persons to express feelings, share ideas, and ask questions. Place on the walls posters and pictures representing different beliefs and symbols. Play meditative music. Set chairs in a semicircle facing a table on which there is a display of different kinds of symbols, such as the following:

- Objects: keys, chalice, coffee cup, wallet, cross, Bible

- Names/persons: Moses, Jesus, George Washington, Helen Keller, Jerusalem

- Statements: Apostles' Creed, U.S. Constitution, U.S. flag salute

- Actions/rituals: Last Supper, football game, national anthem

- Stories: Genesis 1, "Sleeping Beauty," life of Lincoln

- Tastes: slice of bread, coffee, wine

- Smells: incense, flowers

- Sounds: prayer bell, tape of sacred chants

Provide instructions both on newsprint and orally as participants enter the room. Ask them to look at the display and choose one symbol that carries some significant meaning for them personally, but to leave the symbol on the display. Allow time for persons to look and choose until the music concludes. After each person has selected a symbol, invite individuals (including the leaders) to share their choice and tell something about its meaning for them. The experience can be summarized by noting the different kinds of symbols and by relating some of the meanings expressed by the participants to the following definition of symbol (printed on a poster):

> A true metaphor or symbol is more than a sign, it is a bearer of the reality to which it refers. The hearer not only learns about that reality, but participates in it, and is invaded by it.[5]

Symbols and Perspectives of Faith

To provide a conceptual frame for understanding how symbols might be interpreted, participants can now encounter or review how each of the four perspectives understands the subject area "Symbol." Table 10 reproduces the four adult perspectives on symbol listed in table 2 (chapter 1, pages 22–23).

As the participants review the four perspectives, have them brainstorm the advantages and disadvantages of each perspective's understanding of symbol. For example, they might mention the following:

- *Perspective A:* investment of feeling vs. limited scope

- *Perspective B:* awareness of different meanings vs. lack of communal grounding and analysis

- *Perspective C:* ability to analyze any symbol vs. impatience with some of the other perspectives (e.g., A's valuing of feelings)

---

5. This modified definition is taken from Amos N. Wilder, *Early Christian Rhetoric: The Language of the Gospel* (Cambridge: Harvard University Press, 1964), 84.

Table 10
Faith Perspectives on Symbol

Symbol (persons, objects, stories, things, etc.)	Perspective A Refers to an abstract and personal reality to which it is bound; cannot be changed without changing the reality. Emotive bonding with symbol	Perspective B Has multiple meanings; refers to an abstract reality to which it is bound. A bonding with the symbol and its reality through one's feelings and preferences	Perspective C Rationally separated from the conceptual reality to which it refers. Rational but passionate bonding to the conceptual reality	Perspective D Joined with the reality and one's feelings and ideas into a new vision. Emotional-rational-aesthetic bonding
Example: a national flag	Harming the flag harms the country itself; there can be deep emotions about flag-burning, wearing the flag, for instance, as though one desecrates the very nation to which the flag is bound.	Feelings depend on how important the nation and flag are to the individual, what the individual feels like doing.	The flag *represents* the nation; there can be strong feelings about showing disrespect for the flag and what it represents, but they are not bound together as at perspective A.	The flag as symbol is important and can evoke strong feelings, but the reality is the nation and the vision that it tries to embody.

- *Perspective D:* integrative understanding vs. rejection of rationalizations

To become familiar with and to work with these definitions, participants can read the following short story (on page 100) and its interpretation, and identify different faith perspectives that are represented.[6]

In participants' analysis of "The Green Atlas," the symbol and the reality or meaning it holds for the persons in the story can be related to the perspectives of faith. The young David represents perspective A by equating the tree with the forest he loves. They are inseparable and bound together by his feelings for the tree and for his grandfather. The forest ranger represents perspective C by separating the symbol from the concept it represents. That is, he can destroy the symbol (cut down the tree) while preserving the concept (the forest itself). We can see David shifting to perspective B by picking a new seedling that then has a special and different meaning for him. It is also possible that perspective D is represented in the final state-

---

6. The story is derived from the *Mennonite*, January 29, 1980, 68ff.

The Green Atlas

Briefly, the story concerns itself with our young hero, David, who fears for the well-being of his grandfather's favorite tree — a giant, majestic pine that appears to be holding up the sky (a green Atlas). David shares in the meaning of this tree as a symbol of the forest that he learned to love during walks with his beloved grandfather, a man whose youthful ambitions had fostered the huge Brewster Lumber Company that bore his name. The reputation of this company — epitomizing a genuine concern for the forest and the conservation of this important resource — was a reflection of the influence of this same man who had watched a chosen, promising seedling grow into this impressive symbol of that which meant so much to him.

Now, still grieving the death of this beloved grandfather, David discovers to his dismay that the green Atlas is destined for cutting down. He intercepts the forest ranger in his purposeful stride toward the tree for marking it, and there — under the protective arms of that great symbol — pleads his case for its survival in a voice ragged with grief.

The gentle but firm forest ranger helps David see the tree in a scope and a depth beyond his previous comprehension. David learns that this symbol of the forest — this grand, majestic, meaningful, almost protective symbol — has become a threat, a detriment to the many little trees that are to carry the forest forward in its dynamic development. If the symbol of the forest concept (the green Atlas) endangers the reality of the concept (the forest itself and all it implies), then the symbol must give way.

We can share with David the uncertainty of action even if we agree with the finding. It is difficult to think of our most cherished symbols as the tree(s) that keep us from seeing the forest. Such symbols seem to be a focal point, something tangible to which to tie values and which make those values more apparent and accessible.

Historically, the Christian church has rallied to many symbols, often of great benefit toward unity and singleness of purpose. Unfortunately, their earlier commendable meanings were sometimes used to justify or camouflage acts of dubious virtue. (The cross of the Crusades is perhaps one of the more glaring examples.)

The story suggests a possible contrast (a beautiful one) to the weaknesses described. David has to give up the green Atlas (he even sees the wisdom of that action, eventually), but that does not mean he has to give up the concept that it represented for his forefather. David must now make this concept his own; he must make the faith of his forebears his own faith.

To help him grapple with faith in an intangible ideal, David does as his grandfather had done. He chooses his own symbol. He finds his own small pine seedling that will grow as he grows, helping to hold up his overarching "sky" of values. David is thrilled with the thought that, being so close to the green Atlas, his seedling might in fact have seeded from that majestic symbol.

What a beautiful thought this suggests! Our faith, like the forest of the story, is an ongoing entity. Our views of symbols that were applicable to another time may have to be updated to our time and concerns, but they will not be foreign to the faith nor to the previous symbol. Our faith must be rooted in our spiritual history — the concept of the forest must go on. Perhaps we, too, as did the David of our story, can thrill to the thought that our new symbols or our new appraisal of the old ones can "seed" from our ethnic and cultural symbols and traditions.

ment, which integrates the old and the new in the context of community and traditions.

In "The Green Atlas," David "believes" that the green Atlas was "the forest that he learned to love during walks with his beloved grandfather." The ranger "believes" that the "symbol of the forest... has become a threat, a detriment to the many little trees that are to carry the forest forward in its dynamic development." Ways of thinking about symbols such as the green Atlas correlate with ways of thinking about beliefs. The four perspectives of faith help us understand how persons might agree that they believe in the same words or images but disagree about what that belief means. For example, persons may agree that they believe "the Bible is inspired by God" but disagree about what that means to them. Compare the description of each perspective's understanding of "Symbol" in table 10 with the following statements taken from our research. These statements can be shared with participants by asking them to identify and give reasons for those perspectives they prefer and those they do not prefer.

Perspective A personally and tacitly connects the belief and its true meaning: "I think in most cases scriptures were probably divinely inspired; that is a belief of mine. I don't know that I can give you a reason for that. ["Inspired by God"] means that the person who actually wrote the physical words down went inside of himself, herself, and was inspired, was found within the words that got written down."

For perspective B, personal feelings and preferences color the way one thinks about the inspiration of the Bible:

See, what I believe is that God inspires a person when he wants to write something down. Therefore, that person will write it down, but he will write it down that way he wants to do it, the way he sees the situation. . . . God says only, more or less, . . . "You see this point this way, you go ahead and write it the way you feel, what you want to see."

Perspective C understands belief rationally and conceptually: " 'Inspired by God' means that it comes from a conviction, a conscious awareness that what is being said, that what the author, what they are writing is universal, that it comes from their relationship with God."

Perspective D rejoins belief with feelings and ideas into a new vision:

["Inspired by God"] means that people who are engaged in reflection on the meaning of relationship with God, with life, with life together, see their understanding reflected back to them in terms of a vision they have about God and life together, so that to be inspired by God is to have responded to a call to be in relationship with God, to be in dialogue in matters of faith. . . to be apprehended by a vision and to be intending to understand what that vision means for concrete persons trying to live life together in faith.

Similar perspectival characteristics can be expected in the way persons communicate their beliefs in God, as these formulated responses exemplify:

- *Perspective A:* God is personal, like a friend or loving father (as is the father in the parable of the prodigal son). God is the one who cares for and protects us. Or God is like a judge or punishing father (as some persons interpreted the God of the Old Testament as a God of wrath). God may be forgiving, or God may remind us of our sin and guilt and punish us if we do not repent continually.

- *Perspective B:* God is what anybody feels personally that God should be.

- *Perspective C:* God is personal but generally interpreted in terms of more abstract and conceptual meanings. God is the God of justice or human liberation. God is the eternal Creator who shows no partiality, because God's sun shines on both the evil and the good.

- *Perspective D:* God is an all-encompassing reality, that power of love in which we live and move and have our being. God's reign or kingdom is both a living presence and a shaping vision of justice and peace for all reality, which persons are invited to embrace with all their heart, mind, soul, and strength.

Beliefs and Transformation

Perspectives of faith on beliefs can be deepened and enriched by offering persons different ways they might think about their own beliefs, for example, regarding the inspiration of the Bible or images for God. Other possibilities for facilitating transformation for each perspective include the following:

- *Perspective A:* experiencing alternative meanings or rituals without negating the original emotional bonding; extending the original meaning, for example, by looking at several ways of understanding a favorite hymn or trying different modes for personal prayer

- *Perspective B:* being exposed to different interpretations of one belief and exploring reasons for them without dichotomizing them as right or wrong; or assessing the relative adequacy of different interpretations, such as the difference between a private or communal understanding of church

- *Perspective C:* role-taking the effect of "breaking" beliefs or symbols (i.e., demythologizing them) on persons representing perspective A, hence exploring the importance of feelings; expanding the conceptual possibilities of a belief's meaning

- *Perspective D:* living, reflecting on, dialoguing about, and reassessing personal commitment to a belief; or moving the partiality of the belief's meaning by exploring the universals to which it and other religions' beliefs point

These examples could themselves plant seeds of change if used as part of a discussion about what might foster or hinder transformation of different perspectives of faith about beliefs and symbols.

A Word of Caution

Because a strong emotional bond links symbols or beliefs with their realities for Affiliating Al and Bargaining Betty, when their symbols and beliefs are analyzed, realities are changed. For these perspectives, changes in the worship setting (e.g., rearranging the pulpit and table) or rational explanations of a belief (e.g., the virgin birth) could be likened to moving the furniture in heaven or breaking the stone tablets. Religious leaders need to put themselves in the place of persons using these perspectives when contemplating changes in the church. Often the most effective method of introducing potential changes is to help persons expand their perceptions by offering several optional ways of thinking about a belief. Or, similarly, one might provide different ways of experiencing a practice or belief such as Communion.

It is important to reiterate our caution against labeling persons. For example, because of the strong emotional component of many symbols and beliefs, persons may tend to encapsulate their understandings of a particular symbol or belief. In other words, they may sound like Affiliating Al when describing their fondness for a certain picture of Jesus but actually function most of the time like Conceptualizing Charles. In short, efforts to enrich perspectives of faith about symbols and beliefs are most likely to succeed when the praxis of Christian nurture is grounded in understanding and respect for the intrinsic worth of all persons and their perspectives of faith.

9

NURTURING FAITH PERSPECTIVES ON CHURCH

There is no longer Jew or Greek, there is no longer slave or free, there is no longer male and female; for all of you are one in Christ Jesus.
— Galatians 3:28 NRSV

Different portrayals of the church as community are primary examples of the diversity of belief that has characterized Christianity since its earliest beginnings. Then as now, Christians have generated various images of their communal identity as followers of Jesus or believers in Christ. Followers of the earthly peasant Jesus may have understood themselves as a gathering within Jewish and Roman cultures dedicated "to rebuild[ing] a society upward from its grass roots, but on principles of religious and economic egalitarianism, with free healing brought directly to the peasant homes and free sharing of whatever they had in return."[1] The apostle Paul attempted to build up faith communities (e.g., in Thessalonica and Corinth) as the "body of Christ" by helping them distinguish themselves from their culture through independence (1 Thess. 4:11–12) or upright conduct (1 Cor. 5, 6). The faith community addressed in 1 Peter 2:9–17 adopted the image of God's special people in exile to empower a vocation of honorable and accommodating civil behavior, so that the nations might "glorify God on the day of visitation" (v. 12 RSV). In contrast, John of Patmos encouraged the churches of Asia Minor to be holy communities set apart in order to resist oppression and conquer the enticements of their respective cultures.[2] Throughout its history, the church has found value in each of these contrasting images.

Many contemporary Christian educators are emphasizing congregational education that holds in similar creative tension (1) the nurture of

---

1. John Dominic Crossan, *Jesus: A Revolutionary Biography* (San Francisco: HarperSan-Francisco, 1994), 196.
2. See Keith A. Russell, *In Search of the Church: New Testament Images for Tomorrow's Congregations* (Bethesda, Md.: Alban Institute, 1994), for a readable and noncritical discussion of this and other images.

persons into communities of faith, and (2) the vocation[3] that the church as been "called out" to be and to do in the world.[4] The congregation's dual task of building up the Christian community and living out its faith in service to society requires its members to adjudicate differences of opinion about what it means to be a community and what the community's vocation ought to be. These differences become more challenging for pastors and educators when they take into account the four perspectives of faith, which understand church as community in quite different ways. That is, even if every person in a congregation agreed that the congregation should adopt the communal image of "body of Christ," persons' ways of understanding and hence discussing and living out that image would differ. In this chapter, we explore faith perspectives on church as community and on its vocation in the world, and then offer suggestions for enhancing community by focusing on a shaping vision.

Faith Perspectives on Church and Vocation

Faith perspectives on church and vocation can be related to ways of thinking about community and society. Table 11 on the following page summarizes perspectives for the subject area "Community/Society" and provides a frame of reference for composing descriptions of the four perspectives of faith on church as a community with a vocation.

Each of the perspectives will undoubtedly result in varying opinions about the church. Each also represents a distinctive way of thinking about the church's vocation in the world.

For Affiliating Al, the church might be a group of people who believe the same things and who should get along with one another. The church should be a family in which everyone loves each other. Or, Al might think of the

---

3. We have chosen the term *vocation* to highlight the church's active stance toward pursuing justice in the world and also to discontinue the negative connotations of the term *mission* with respect to colonization and conquest. See George E. Tinker, *Missionary Conquest: The Gospel and Native American Cultural Genocide* (Minneapolis: Fortress, 1993). For examples of the use of *vocation* among contemporary religious educators, see James W. Fowler, *Becoming Adult, Becoming Christian: Adult Development and Christian Faith* (San Francisco: Harper & Row, 1984); Maria Harris, *Fashion Me a People: Curriculum in the Church* (Louisville, Ky.: Westminster/John Knox, 1989); and Jack L. Seymour, Margaret Ann Crain, and Joseph V. Crockett, *Educating Christians: The Intersection of Meaning, Learning, and Vocation* (Nashville: Abingdon, 1993).

4. For a similar emphasis upon the congregation's dual character of being a community and being in vocation or mission, see the challenging books by Loren B. Mead, *The Once and Future Church: Reinventing the Congregation for a New Mission Frontier* (Bethesda, Md.: Alban Institute, 1991) and *Transforming Congregations for the Future* (Bethesda, Md.: Alban Institute, 1994); Mary Boys, ed., *Education for Citizenship and Discipleship* (Cleveland: Pilgrim, 1989); and Nelle Slater, ed., *Tensions between Citizenship and Discipleship: A Case Study* (Cleveland: Pilgrim, 1989). Note also the faith community approach to Christian education by Christian educators such as John H. Westerhoff III, *Living the Faith Community: The Church That Makes a Difference* (Minneapolis: Winston, 1985); and Charles R. Foster, *Educating Congregations: The Future of Christian Education* (Nashville: Abingdon, 1994).

Table 11
Faith Perspectives on Community and Society

Community/ society	Affiliating Al	Bargaining Betty	Conceptualizing Charles	Dialectical Donna
	Affectional groups that exclude people who are different	Multiple affectional groups. Aligns with group according to preferences; tolerates others if they are not coercive	Structured by laws, rules, sanctions that maintain the society and its values; exclusive	Open, inclusive; created through social contract, due process

church as a group of persons who do not act on what they believe. In short, he might think of the church stereotypically as a bunch of hypocrites. For Al, there is no clear perception of church as an institutional, connective system.

Al might think that the church's vocation should be to take specific and immediate action for persons as individuals — for the weak, the poor, and the oppressed. Or, Al might think that the church's vocation means the building up of its own faith community through worship, education, proclamation, and fellowship.

For Bargaining Betty, the church is a group of people who feel the same way about God, worship, and values. According to her perspective, other folks can form a church according to what they feel is right. One person's church is as good as anyone else's. Betty may think that no church should force its values on other churches.

Like Al, Betty thinks that the church's vocation should be to take action on behalf of the needy, but she will claim that there is no one right way to go about the church's vocation. Some churches might engage in concrete forms of charity, whereas others might see their vocation in terms of nurturing and supporting their own. To Betty, it all depends on what each church prefers, because she is uncertain as to why one might be more valid than another.

For Conceptualizing Charles, the church is constituted by people who subscribe to a common belief system that is expressed through the formation of the church as an institution. He affirms the need to maintain the institution through its polity and creeds in order to prevent any breakdown of the system and its values. Charles tends to stereotype other church systems, and he excludes church systems that constitute a threat to his own.

According to Charles's perspective, the church may represent itself as an institution engaged in the transformation of society or set apart from society. Hence, the church's vocation might be shaped by a concern to counter basic causes of injustice, as well as by the need to change political, societal, or ecclesiastical social systems. Or, the church's vocation might be shaped by its duty to defend the faith against society's assaults on its values.

For Dialectical Donna, the church may be a community of persons who embody interdependence, openness, and inclusivity. These are values grounded in its common covenant with God, the all-encompassing reality and power of love in which all persons live and move and have their being. Or, Donna may think that the church incarnates a "scandal of particularity" in which commitment to particular symbols and rituals is in paradoxical tension with commitment to universal visions of community.

According to Donna's perspective, the church's vocation is shaped by its commitment to God, whose unbounded love holds all persons to be of equal and intrinsic value. Donna might think that the church should seek to become an inclusive community of interdependence, composed of diverse and growing persons who derive their vision from Christ and who then model inclusivity within society. Or, she might think that the church should be engaged in transforming society into a more just, inclusive, and interdependent social system. Perhaps she would think that both of these understandings of the church and its vocation should be integrated into an as-yet-unknown synergy with other religions' images of fulfillment.

A Shaping Vision of Community and Vocation

One of the most difficult problems to be addressed by any attempt to affirm diversity is that of establishing and articulating some commonality that enables people to work together but that does not erase or compromise authentic, and possibly insurmountable, differences. Most congregations represent a wide range of opinions as well as a mixture of identifying characteristics such as gender, age, race, and so forth. Perspectives of faith can shed some light on how those differences are understood. In addition to increasing mutual understanding, however, it is necessary to orient a community to a shared vision of its vocation in the world.

To illustrate the possibilities and difficulties for a congregation adopting a shaping vision of community, we'll consider the vision of community presented in Ephesians 4:1–16. Using the same translation as was used in chapter 7 (NRSV), we'll identify five major concepts of this vision and discuss how each perspective might interpret them.[5]

> [1]I therefore, the prisoner in the Lord, beg you to lead a life worthy of the calling to which you have been called, [2]with all humility and gentleness, with patience, bearing with one another in love, [3]making every effort to maintain the unity of the Spirit in the bond of peace.

---

5. For a detailed analysis of this biblical text, see Everding, Snelling, and Wilcox, "A Shaping Vision of Community."

[4]There is one body and one Spirit, just as you were called to the one hope of your calling, [5]one Lord, one faith, one baptism, [6]one God and Father of all, who is above all and through all and in all.

[7]But each of us was given grace according to the measure of Christ's gift. [8]Therefore it is said,

"When he ascended on high he made captivity itself a captive;
he gave gifts to his people."

[9]When it says, *"He ascended,"* what does it mean but that he had also descended into the lower parts of the earth? [10]He who descended is the same one who ascended far above all the heavens, so that he might fill all things. [11]The *gifts he gave* were that some would be apostles, some prophets, some evangelists, some pastors and teachers, [12]to equip the saints for the work of ministry, for building up the body of Christ, [13]until all of us come to the unity of the faith and of the knowledge of the Son of God, to maturity, to the measure of the full stature of Christ. [14]We must no longer be children, tossed to and fro and blown about by every wind of doctrine, by people's trickery, by their craftiness in deceitful scheming. [15]But speaking the truth in love, we must grow up in every way into him who is the head, into Christ, [16]from whom the whole body, joined and knit together by every ligament with which it is equipped, as each part is working properly, promotes the body's growth in building itself up in love.

1. *Relational and unitary values:* The writer's opening exhortation to "lead a life worthy of the calling" specifies relational values and behaviors (e.g., humility, gentleness, patience, bearing one another in love, maintaining unity, peace) grounded on the community's creedal affirmation of the unity upon which it is based (vv. 4–6). In verses 15–16, the writer identifies love as the cardinal relational value and behavior that contributes to the body's growth in and toward that unity of faith.

2. *Individual worth:* Each individual is valued as a recipient of a measure of "grace" given as "Christ's gift" (v. 7). In verse 8, the writer cites Psalm 68:18, first, to ground the authority attributed to Christ as the one who "descended" to give gifts, because he is the one who "ascended . . . so that he might fill all things" (v. 10; cf. Eph. 1:9–10, 23; 3:9–11, 18–19). Second, the writer capitalizes on the word *gifts* to list the gifted types of individuals (v. 11) and their comprehensive function "to equip the saints for the work of ministry" (v. 12).

3. *Body of Christ:* The writer clarifies the "work of ministry" as "building up the body of Christ" (v. 12). Two behavioral characteristics that contribute to this "building up" are identified: "speaking the truth in love" (v. 15) and "each part . . . promot[ing] the body's growth in building itself up in love" (v. 16).

4. *Growth in transcendence:* The process of the body's growth leads to "maturity," which is pictured, but not defined, with images of "the unity of the faith and of the knowledge of the Son of God" and "the full stature of Christ" (v. 13). These images lure the body to transcend diversity, the partiality of its knowledge, and complacency. Hence, the community is continually encouraged to "no longer be children" but rather to "grow up in every way into him who is the head, into Christ" (vv. 14–15).

5. *Shared authority:* Although identified at first as one who exhorts as "the prisoner in the Lord" (v. 1), the writer relinquishes authority by identifying his function as just one of the gifted functions (such as apostle or teacher). The writer also notes that the work of ministry is that of the saints (i.e., the whole community) and explicitly includes himself in the growth process (using "we" in vv. 14–15).

Perspectival Interpretations of the Vision

If a congregation were to adopt this text for its shaping vision of community, there would undoubtedly be different ways of interpreting these five concepts. So, even though the text places high value on unity, a diversity of interpretations is the first matter to acknowledge. The following descriptions of how the four perspectives might interpret the images and ideas identified in the preceding section expand upon our initial grid and discussion of this text in chapter 7.

Affiliating Al: Perspective A

1. Love as the cardinal *relational and unitary value* is seen in terms of a focus on interpersonal relationships based in feelings: "How can I love someone I don't like?" There is stereotyping and rejection of those whom Al doesn't like or approve. Interpersonal ties are enduring and not to be disrupted.

2. *Individual worth* is based on being good according to the values of Al's group.

3. The *body of Christ,* the church, is composed of those who love and care for each other and who maintain unity by preventing dissension. Those who do not fit, who are not "like us," or who are disruptive are excluded.

4. *Growth in transcendence* is understood as following Christ's example of what it means to be a good Christian or disciple of Christ: embodying positive attitudes, loving feelings, and right beliefs.

5. *Shared authority* is possible if all persons can demonstrate the personal qualities that the group itself sanctions. If not, then only persons who have those qualities should be leaders.

Bargaining Betty: Perspective B

1. Love as the cardinal *relational and unitary value* is also understood in terms of interpersonal relationships based in feelings, but love may include tolerance of those who may "feel" differently about who they are and what they believe, as long as they don't try to force those understandings on Betty. If they do use coercion, then she will reject them.

2. *Individual worth* is based on how the group feels about an individual or how the individual feels about the group, even if the individual doesn't fit all the values of the group.

3. The *body of Christ* includes those whose hearts are in accord with the way Betty's church feels, but some who may not feel that way can be included as long as they do not disrupt Betty's community and its good relationships.

4. *Growth in transcendence* is understood as living toward the ideal of what Betty's group feels is the best way to be a Christian today: embodying loving attitudes, tolerance for other persons, and a Christianity that "works for us."

5. *Shared authority* is possible if the group feels that it can work together to build itself as a community. If persons in the group do not want to share leadership, then they should not be required to do so.

Conceptualizing Charles: Perspective C

1. Love as the cardinal *relational and unitary value* is understood as a value more fundamental than feelings and interpersonal dynamics. We can love those we neither know nor like, if their value systems are similar to ours.

2. *Individual worth* is based on the values of an institution and on the individual's contribution to it.

3. The *body of Christ* is a structured organization whose major purpose is to maintain its values as expressed through laws, doctrine, tradition, and so forth.

4. *Growth in transcendence* means to live under the moral imperatives of the kingdom of God or the eschatological Christ. The community is continually called to regulate and maintain its life according to the will and purposes of God in Christ.

5. *Shared authority* is a possibility if the system defines the criteria of authority in such a way that all persons can have some voice. Otherwise, authority should be located in the persons who are the credentialed representatives of the system.

Dialectical Donna: Perspective D

1. Love as the cardinal *relational and unitary value* is understood as valuing all persons equally. Love does not depend solely on positive emotions or on an institution's shared values.

2. *Individual worth* of each life is intrinsic and independent of limiting criteria.

3. The *body of Christ* is an interdependent community composed of diverse and growing persons who derive their vision from Christ. Acceptance of all persons makes it possible to speak the truth in love for each person and for the whole body. If one falters, the whole body suffers.

4. *Growth in transcendence* involves holding in tension the experience of the immanent Christ, who stands with us in our daily existence, and the lure of the transcendent Christ, who beckons the faithful to pursue the unseen beyond the seen. From that standpoint, we should be prepared to evaluate and transform any existing form and set of beliefs of the church.

5. *Shared authority* is possible in a community that values inclusivity and establishes covenants to protect and honor equally the value of each person.

Interpretations in Dialogue

Given these ways of interpreting five major concepts in Ephesians 4:1–16, is it any wonder that congregations require long, heavily debated, and often frustrated processes to compose vision statements of their own? The process can be even more complex when matters such as temperament, age, experience, social location, and other dynamics are taken into account. Yet each perspective identifies distinctive values that contribute to a rich collage of options to be considered. For example, consider the hypothetical discussion of a committee considering how its congregation might understand itself as the body of Christ.

> DONNA: The image of the body of Christ shapes my understanding of our congregation as an inclusive community. For Paul, to be in Christ meant there was neither Jew nor Greek, slave nor free, male nor female, so we can honor all persons regardless of their age, color, gender, sexual orientation, and class. I'd like to see that as part of our vision statement.

> BETTY: I can go along with that up to a point. What if some handicapped person continually disrupts our worship service, or a homeless person wants to use our kitchen and sleep in one of our classrooms? I can be tolerant up to a point.

> AL$_a$: I agree. Doesn't being the body of Christ mean that we love one another? What will such people really contribute to our fellowship? I think we need some guidelines. We can't be open to just anybody.

> AL$_b$: I don't know about that. Jesus cared for the outcasts of his day. I feel that we should take care of the homeless and handicapped. If they want to be part of our church, then that's the loving thing to do.

CHARLES: Can we at least begin to develop some criteria and a clear statement about our vision? Maybe it would help if we looked at our denomination's polity about what we can and cannot do. Maybe some clear criteria can help us determine what people need to affirm in order to align themselves with this church.

DONNA: But are we really confined to a polity and limiting criteria in light of Christ's valuing of each individual because of his or her intrinsic worth? As the text says, "Each of us was given grace." Can't we go beyond the limits and guidelines of what our denomination says is allowable?

AL$_a$: What does polity have to do with anything? Aren't we to be loving and good as Christ was?

AL$_b$: I agree. Do we really need to spell out everything?

CHARLES: Well, the author of Ephesians certainly did, especially if you read the rest of the letter after 4:16. I think we need to be systematic about how we go about this. Loving and caring are OK, but we need to qualify those virtues in terms of what's best for our church as an institution. Confessions of faith identify those who share a common allegiance.

BETTY: That's OK with me, but people do have different opinions. We need to be tolerant and not fix everything in some sort of ironclad definition.

Will this committee ever come to agreement? The lengthy history of the church in the world would suggest that committees like this one often do.

A Vision's Challenge

The vision of community projected in Ephesians 4:1–16 can function as an invitation to each perspective to acknowledge and relate to others for the sake of an enlarged understanding of what it means to be a community of faith. It presents for interpretation and reflection such content as love; the relationship between individual and group worth; the congregation as a body; authority; and the interactive growth of persons and communities. This vision also provides the opportunity for a congregation to engage in what Parker Palmer identifies as "an education in transcendence." In Ephesians 4, the transcendent Christ is named but not defined as the shaping vision of "unity of faith and knowledge," "maturity," and "full stature." Christ invites individuals in community to grow and work together, "to see beyond appearances into the hidden realities of life — beyond facts into truth, beyond self-interest into compassion, beyond our flagging energies and nagging despairs into the love required to renew the community of creation."[6] Ephesians 4:1–16 is a shaping vision of a community of disciples, those who follow Christ as an example, an ideal, a moral imperative, a lure to see the unseen beyond the seen. Persons in each faith perspective can have the awareness of being caught up in something greater than themselves.

Conclusion

Congregational life is rich in diversity and, hence, in possibilities. As individual congregations struggle to understand and embody what they claim to be as a community with a vocation, we affirm the creative utilization of that diversity. It will never go away! Instead, the Spirit works through the babble of differing opinions and perspectives to create the possibility that persons will say, "In our own languages we hear them speaking about God's deeds of power" (Acts 2:11 NRSV).

---

6. Parker J. Palmer, *To Know as We Are Known: A Spirituality of Education* (San Francisco: Harper & Row, 1983), 13.

10

NURTURING FAITH PERSPECTIVES ON JUSTICE

But let justice roll down like waters,
and righteousness like an ever-flowing stream.

— Amos 5:24 NRSV

As Christians called to live a faithful life in the midst of an often chaotic, violent, impersonal world, one of our greatest needs is to be capable of making ethical decisions about justice issues in ways that demonstrate responsible use of theology, biblical interpretation, critical thinking, and self-awareness of our functioning values. When we trivialize or ignore justice issues in daily life, we are soon overcome with feelings of powerlessness. When justice is made a priority within the church, Christians are nurtured in their abilities to discern and work for just solutions in their congregations and in their world.

Not surprisingly, diversity in definitions of justice complicates our efforts to nurture persons in relation to justice issues. Some definitions of justice include

- impartial adjustment of conflicting claims

- assignment of merited rewards and punishments — being fair

- giving each person her or his due

- sorting out what belongs to whom and returning it accordingly

- quality of conforming to positive law and to divine or natural laws

- what is right

The concepts of impartiality, of right and wrong, of who deserves what — all of these draw upon a number of other orienting beliefs held by each of us: our valuing of persons, our concept of what makes a "good" person, our relationship to law and society, and our perception of universal principles. Given this diversity of understandings of justice and related values, what does it mean to "let justice roll down like waters"?

Faith Perspectives on Justice

Research in perspectives of faith offers one way to organize many of the diverse understandings of justice. As we have said previously, perspectives refer to the cognitive *structures* that underlie persons' organization of various *contents*, or definitions of justice. We will first elaborate the central features of each perspective's understanding of justice (table 12), and then we will introduce one way to nurture deeper understandings of justice through Bible study.

Table 12
Perspectives of Faith on Justice

Justice	Perspective A	Perspective B	Perspective C	Perspective D
(what is right)	Good intentions, right feelings, conformity to conventional images of good behavior	Conformity to conventional images of good behavior; tolerance for people who do not conform, if they have good intentions and do not impose behavior on others	Maintenance of "our" systems and their values, responsibility to the system (church, society), contributions to society	Universal principles, equality of basic rights, equal worth of all persons; a balance of moral and legal points of view

Understanding these four perspectives can help us become more aware of the sources of our own decisions and actions, as well as providing some clues about communicating and working with others who think differently but who share our desire for a just world.

For Affiliating Al, justice is awarded to persons or groups on the basis of how similar their values are to those of the decision makers, and to the "unfortunate" if they deserve it by living according to those same values. What is just is determined by good intentions, good feelings ("It makes me feel good to help"), or conformity to conventional images of virtuous behavior ("Good persons help deserving people who are less fortunate"). Al understands social justice as charity rather than as working to change social structures. Here are some examples of Al's reasoning:

- One who steals should be punished because he or she is being selfish or greedy.

- One who steals should not be punished if his or her intentions are good.

- We should be willing to help those on welfare, because they cannot help it if they are poor.

- We should not help those on welfare, because most of them are just lazy.

Bargaining Betty is very similar to Al, but she is more tolerant of diversity. People are entitled to their own values, as long as they do not impose them on others. How one feels about something is important. These are some examples:

- It is not up to me to judge whether or not a person should be punished for stealing. It depends on that person's own values, whether he thinks he needs something that badly.

- We should help people on welfare, because they have a right to live the way they want to.

- We should not help people on welfare, because they don't want to work, and helping them has a bad influence on others.

For Conceptualizing Charles, justice is awarded on the basis of whether or not one contributes to the chosen system (society, church, corporation). If one subscribes to the values of that system and conforms to the laws, doctrines, assumptions, and taboos of that system, he or she is doing what is right. Justice is understood as the maintenance of "our" systems and their values and legal rights. Justice is that which contributes to the system or the common good, or that which recognizes the possibility of higher moral laws. Social justice includes the possibility of changing social structures. Here are some examples:

- If one steals, one must be responsible enough to accept the legal consequences.

- Stealing should be punished in order to give respect to property rights.

- Stealing may be justified if it is done in response to higher laws.

- We should help those on welfare, because it is the problems of our society that have created the situation in which they find themselves.

- We should not help those on welfare, because they are not contributing to society; they are not taking responsibility.

For Dialectical Donna, all persons are seen as individuals with dignity and intrinsic worth, as ends in themselves rather than as means to other ends. Justice is awarded through the balancing of moral and legal points of view, rather than on the basis of whether or not persons or groups fit into stereotypes or value systems. Donna understands the need to change social structures in light of values such as these. Consider these examples:

- Whether or not a person should be punished for stealing should be determined on the basis of basic rights that are being denied.

- We could be justified in helping those on welfare when we look at the whole situation, the context in which some of them grew up, the situations of deprivation that exist, and our own commitments. The right to a decent life (food, shelter, clothing, medical care, being treated with dignity) is top priority for each citizen.

- When the welfare system is abused to the extent that it infringes on the basic rights of others, it must be closely examined and safeguards built in to protect the rights of all.

Nurturing Faith Perspectives on Justice through Bible Study

The following Bible study contributes to persons' ethical decision making by helping them explore their understandings of justice in dialogue with an image of justice in the Bible and with different adult perspectives on justice.

Opening the Session

After participants are welcomed and a brief prayer is offered, invite them to look at pictures of Martin Luther King Jr., Mahatma Gandhi, and Mother Teresa. Ask them to share their feelings about one of the persons and the image of justice that person represents to them. After receiving these responses, state the session's purpose (and also write it on newsprint or chalkboard): to explore an image of justice in the Bible (Micah 6:8) and to reflect on new insights about justice to which God might be leading us.

Interpreting Micah 6:8

The purpose of this part of the session is to listen to what the text says and to consider what it may have meant in its own time. This may be a small or large group activity structured using the tasks that follow.

WHAT DOES THE TEXT SAY?

> He has told you, O mortal, what is good;
> and what does the Lord require of you
> but to do justice, and to love kindness,
> and to walk humbly with your God?
> (Mic. 6:8 NRSV)

1. Who is speaking in Micah 6:1–2? (See Micah 1:1.)

2. To whom is 6:8 addressed? (See 1:1–2; 6:2b.)

3. In 6:2, the speaker mentions a "controversy" or "case" or "lawsuit" (depending on the translation). Who are the "characters" or "parties" involved in this controversy?

4. In 6:3–5, one of the parties to the controversy is speaking but is not mentioned by name. From what is said in those verses, who do you think is probably speaking?

5. In 6:6–7, someone else speaks, basically asking a question. Who might this be? (A clue to the identity of this speaker might be found in 6:8a and in the context of the answer to question 2.) What action is this individual proposing to take? (See 6:6a, in particular, but note the rest of 6:6 and 6:7.) What seems to be the purpose of the proposed actions? (See 6:7a.)

6. What have the people done to get involved in this situation? (See 2:1–2; 3:5, 9–11; 6:9–12.)

7. What is the answer to the question given in 6:8?

8. If Micah 6:8 is in the form of a lawsuit, who would be the accuser? the judge? the defendant?

WHAT DID THE TEXT MEAN IN ITS TIME?

Have the participants read the following information and then respond to the questions listed below.

With Amos, Hosea, and Isaiah, Micah was one of the four eighth-century B.C.E. prophets. His career probably spanned only the last quarter of the eighth century. He lived in a small frontier village about twenty-five miles southwest of Jerusalem. He was preoccupied with social justice and was unafraid of princes, prophets, and priests. His has been called the voice of the village peasant against the rapacious power of the state. A major theme of his preaching was that religious worship without social justice was meaningless.

In Micah 6:1–8, the prophet uses the image of a lawsuit to illustrate the relationship between God and God's people, who have failed to live up to the covenant. A confession of sin and the making of offerings in hopes of forgiveness are implied in 6:6–7. In 6:8, Micah delivers God's verdict and requirements for the people to be made

right with God once again. This is in the context of the obligations of
the covenant between God and God's people.[1]

1. What were the main issues about which and situations to which
    Micah was speaking?

2. How would you describe the meaning and emphasis of "justice" in
    the verses you have read as they would have been understood at the
    time the text was written?

WHAT DOES THE TEXT MEAN FOR US TODAY?

To complete the process of interpretation, ask the participants to respond
to questions designed to help appropriate meaning from listening to what
the text says and meant in its time. Suggest that participants imagine that
Micah was writing this text to them.

1. How does Micah's message make you feel?

2. Does Micah's message speak to any of your experiences in or obser-
    vations about the world as it is today? If so, in what ways?

3. Do you think Christian social awareness in the United States is
    generally uninformed and innocent? Why or why not?

Ways of Thinking about Justice

This part of the session consists of three steps. First, participants read
descriptions of the four perspectives on justice in table 12 on page 115.
Second, they use this information to enact a role-play. Third, they reflect
on the role-play and on their interpretation of Micah 6:8.

ROLE-PLAY

After participants have read the descriptions in table 12, divide the participants into four groups. Assign each group one of the four adult faith
perspectives (A, B, C, or D), from which they will role-play a response to a
discussion question. The leader will function as chair of a church committee, with participants role-playing the committee by responding from their
assigned perspectives. Give each group the following task.

> Task: We constitute an administrative committee of a local Protes-
> tant, mainly white middle-class congregation. The congregation has
> been given the opportunity to participate with Habitat for Human-
> ity in building a house for a Catholic Mexican family in the area.
> The question for discussion is: "Should our congregation build this
> house?"

---

1. The description is drawn from Walter Brueggemann, Sharon Parks, and Thomas H.
Groome, *To Act Justly, Love Tenderly, Walk Humbly: An Agenda for Ministers* (Mahwah,
N.J.: Paulist, 1986).

Role-plays like this one are more productive and enjoyable when they are conducted with some humor and playfulness. It is also important that participants understand that both pro and con conclusions are found in all perspectives. So, for example, perspective A might be represented by either of the following statements:

- *Pro:* "It would make us feel good to help those people."

- *Con:* "I don't know if those people would fit into our kind of neighborhood."

Encourage each group to explore several reasons their assigned perspective might give for both pro and con answers. After groups have had a chance to talk among themselves about possible responses, the leader or "chair of the committee" calls the mock meeting of the entire group to order and leads a discussion about building the house.[2]

REFLECTION

After the discussion, aid the participants in debriefing and reflecting on the discussion, using the following questions:

1. How did you feel during this exercise?

2. Did anything stand out for you? If so, what?

3. Which perspective or perspectives would you like to see this committee take in working with the issue of support for Habitat for Humanity?

4. What do you think might be some prevailing perspectives on justice in our congregation (without identifying individuals)?

5. How do our differing perspectives on justice relate to our understandings of justice in Micah 6:8?

6. What challenges does this information present to us?

Comments

This study gives participants an opportunity to encounter different perspectives on justice without advocating that one is to be preferred. The study also aims at empowering the participants to make their own interpretations of a biblical text by following a disciplined process. Both of these activities can model various dimensions of justice by (1) affirming participants who engage in the study with good intentions and who do not try to

---

2. Some people find it difficult to role-play any perspective other than their own. An alternative method could engage the group as a whole by asking them to suggest pro and con responses for each perspective. If an answer is given that clearly does not relate to the assigned perspective, help the group try to find where it might fit. Remind participants how difficult it is to "guess" about the perspective of any particular statement.

coerce others into thinking as they do, (2) valuing all who seek to implement the system of questions and tasks designed to aid interpretation and application of scripture, and (3) treating each person and her or his ideas with dignity and respect.

Nurturing Faith Perspectives on Justice through Case Study

Case studies provide persons with another way to clarify their ways of thinking about justice. The following case study deals with the issue of the ordination of women. It can be used as a role-play debate in which participants respond from the four perspectives of faith. Or participants can be divided into groups to discuss the case and to identify negative, positive, and ambivalent positions and reasons. Another option would be to have participants simply read and respond to the case.

The material presented here illustrates that there are more than two sides of an issue. In fact, as we have illustrated in previous chapters, persons may argue pro or con about an issue from each of the four perspectives of faith, making a total of *at least* eight possible positions with regard to a single matter! The important point is that succumbing to conventional pressures to present "two sides" of an issue tends to polarize persons and sets up a win/lose situation. Examining controversial issues from diverse perspectives and identifying various subtexts of the issue can enable commonalities and win/win understandings to emerge.

After the following case study, we provide a profile sketch for each faith perspective. These sketches illustrate the kinds of reasoning we might expect to hear from each perspective on the issue of the ordination of women. The quotations are taken from research in which adults were asked to respond to the case study.

Case Study

You are a member of the board of ministry of a denomination whose polity or law includes the ordination of women. The board is meeting to decide on the ordination of Charles J. It has been determined that, in general, Charles meets the standards of fitness and competence for ministry. However, in discussions with Charles, a major issue has surfaced that raises in the minds of some members of the board an obstacle to his ordination.

Charles has expressed his belief that the church is wrong in ordaining women to the Christian ministry. He believes this practice is contrary to his understanding of the Bible. In response to questions, Charles indicates that he would serve with women who were ordained and he would not seek to prevent the ordination of women, but he could not in conscience vote for the ordination of women or participate in the ordination of women. Some members of the board believe Charles's view so violates the church's understanding of ministry that he should not be ordained. Should the board of ministry ordain Charles? Why or why not?[3]

Responses by Perspectives of Faith

For Affiliating Al, the world is composed of individual relationships, but they are structured on the basis of mutual affection and meaningful continuing relationships. Expressions such as love, doing good, and "helping people to grow" often characterize communication for this perspective. Affectional groups or communities are seen as the definition of society. Al best understands the kinds of feelings and attitudes in others that he himself has experienced and known. *Should the board of ministry ordain Charles? Why or why not?*

- *Yes:* "The church has a ministry to Charles ... so we don't cut him off from his growth. . . . There are other things people do I don't agree with. . . . The loving response to Charles is to accept him."

- *No:* "I can see him having problems so far as women in the church . . . women in leadership roles. . . . I think he is going to have to work that out."

For Bargaining Betty, the world is viewed in terms of interpersonal relationships and multiple meanings. Differences of opinion are evaluated according to how one feels about one's viewpoint. Authority is based on one's preferences. Betty allows for tolerance among diverse opinions, as long as persons do not try to force their views on others. *Should the board of ministry ordain Charles? Why or why not?*

- *Yes:* "Well, we could say that since the church is a pluralistic church and involves people of varying views and opinions, that we can accept most anyone, or we could say that we would hope that we could convince Charles to change his mind."

- *No:* "I guess one of the reasons would be his exclusive attitude. Well, I guess because it seems that, even though we are isolating that one idea . . . he would be excluding half the human race from the ordained ministry, and if it was probably left up to him, [he] could be excluding some good ministers."

For Conceptualizing Charles, the world is composed of explicit rational systems and ideologies. Laws, rules, criteria, and sanctions override interpersonal relationships and help solve conflicting demands and values

---

3. Prepared by Dana W. Wilbanks and H. Edward Everding Jr. for "Decision Making and the Bible," a class taught at the Iliff School of Theology. See also H. Edward Everding Jr. and Dana W. Wilbanks, *Decision Making and the Bible* (Valley Forge, Pa.: Judson, 1975).

among affectional relationships (for example, between family and school, church and business, or political affiliations). Authority is located in the system and its credentialed representatives. Social institutions are viewed solely and exclusively from within those systems. However, Charles has difficulty taking the role of members of social institutions with differing points of view. *Should the board of ministry ordain Charles? Why or why not?*

- *Yes:* "Because of his credentials. He has met the standards of fitness and competency for ministry. He has done all the things the church asked him to do. All it says is that he disagrees with one issue."

- *No:* "It is stated that his denomination's polity includes the ordination of women. This is an important part of his denomination. Church government is a framework in which people are better able to function in the community."

For Dialectical Donna, the world is a pluralistic, ambiguous, or complex unity. With vision, integrative thinking, and commitment, she understands the principles that pertain universally to all persons and to all societies. With the ability to stand outside the system, Donna can affirm the purpose of law and institutional polity to embody and protect human rights through social contract, rather than just to maintain society. Authority is based on the weighing of traditional authorities in a dialectical process. From this perspective, Donna can take the role of persons with other perspectives. *Should the board of ministry ordain Charles ? Why or why not?*

- *Yes:* "For two reasons: the theological question of grace becomes, 'Where do we say yes or no to a person on what they believe?' If I demand the right that other people give me the freedom to think or believe the way I do, then I have to give that right to others. Also, [it's] a question of civil rights... the constitutional freedom to think or believe the way he happens to think. The purpose of church polity would be to help all of us as individuals and as a collective whole move in the direction of the kingdom of God."

- *No:* "Any institution not only has the right but needs to define what it is as an institution... particularly when it is the kind of institution where people contract into it. I think Charles has a perfect right to disagree, but I would question trying to buy into an institution you don't agree with. When his decision of conscience deprives others of a basic right, then the institution is responsible to set limits. Church polity implements in the life of the community what the church stands for."

Comments

Perspectives C and D approach justice issues such as this one with understandings of institutional and principled values and dynamics. The "ethical" dimension of decision making will thus be more complex and, in a sense, more problematic for persons evaluating decisions from these perspectives. This should not negate the valuable insights that perspectives A and B bring to bear on both the situation and the decision. Their approaches will be based more on conventional values and moral reasoning than on ethical principles and reflective analyses. People with perspectives C and D can be reminded of important affectional and conventional values, whereas people with perspectives A and B can be challenged to evaluate situations with criteria appropriate to the issues and values involved in this particular decision.

Conclusion

In this chapter, we have illustrated how the four adult faith perspectives understand justice differently. When dealing with justice issues, therefore, we emphasize that diversity of viewpoints are richer and more complex than the conventionally described "two sides of the issue." Each of the four ways of thinking can respond either pro or con or, for that matter, in a variety of ways between these two extremes. What is important from our standpoint is the pattern of reasoning represented, including the values, norms, and principles appealed to in the process. When persons are not forced into the extremes of pro and con positions and are allowed to explore and express their thinking about an issue in structured environments, then different perspectives stimulate each other and commonalities can emerge in the midst of opposing viewpoints. To "let justice roll down like waters" can be a complex and messy process, but one clearly worthwhile as an experience of the creative dialogue and growth that can take place in the midst of diversity.

11

NURTURING FAITH PERSPECTIVES ON EMPATHY

"In everything do to others as you would have them do to you."
— Matthew 7:12 NRSV

Cultural and religious pluralism confronts us daily in our postmodern world, and diverse understandings of beliefs, church, and justice create misunderstandings within the community of faith. As more and more individuals and underrepresented groups claim their voices, we become more aware of the multiplicity of experience and the relativity of our perspectives and our truth claims. Knowledge of the four faith perspectives can help us understand some of the dynamics of our experience of diversity. At the same time, it assists in our search for common understandings and new ways to create community that honor the integrity of our differences. In this search, we are finding that empathy is an essential quality for building those bridges of understanding.

We understand empathy as the processes of thought involved in putting oneself in the place of the feelings, perspectives, and ideas of another person or group, particularly if these are significantly different from one's own. In cognitive studies, empathy implies primarily role-taking or trying to think the way another person thinks. Empathy is more than sentimental feelings, for it is making the effort to find out what it is really like to walk in another's shoes.

Faith Perspectives on Empathy

The four adult perspectives of faith offer one way to appreciate the different capacities persons may have for taking the role of others. Table 13 on the following page reviews the central features for each of the four perspectives in the area of role-taking.[1]

---

1. For an excellent discussion of role-taking, see Wilcox, *Developmental Journey*. See also Robert L. Selman, *The Growth of Interpersonal Understanding: Developmental and Clinical Analyses* (New York: Academic, 1980).

Table 13
Faith Perspectives on Role-Taking

Role-taking ability	Perspective A	Perspective B	Perspective C	Perspective D
	Based on projection into feelings of others if not too different from oneself; empathy for the "unfortunate," if deserved	Based on tolerance for letting people "do their own thing" as long as they do not impose on others. Understands nonabsolutist perspective, engages in some stereotyping	Based on taking the role of others in context of similar social systems and values	Based on taking the role of persons, groups, other worldviews. Can step outside individual's and system's points of view

Affiliating Al can take the role of others who have similar values and experiences, but it is very difficult for him to put himself in the place of others whose values or experiences are substantially different from his own. He may well have sympathy for the poor, for example, but if he has never experienced poverty, it is easy for him to become judgmental or to stereotype "poor people." He might think about the following persons in these ways:[2]

- Gays and lesbians should not be ordained, because they are separated from God.

- Gays and lesbians should be ordained, because they can do as much good as a heterosexual person.

- We should be nice to liberals [or fundamentalists], because some of them are sincere.

- We should not tolerate liberals [or fundamentalists], because they are judgmental.

Bargaining Betty also tends to stereotype, but she understands that each person should be able to "do his or her own thing," as long as it is not imposed on others. Examples of Betty's role-taking ability include the following:

- Gays and lesbians should be ordained, as long as they are struggling with the problem of sin.

- Gays and lesbians should not be ordained, because they wouldn't feel comfortable in our church.

---

2. The examples of reasoning about the ordination of homosexuals come from a special research project directed by one Iliff School of Theology student, Gregory C. Garland, in 1981.

- Liberals [or fundamentalists] have a right to their own beliefs, as long as they don't bother us.

- Liberals [or fundamentalists] have no right to their beliefs, because they believe they can inflict them on others.

Conceptualizing Charles can recognize that each person is in the context of a social system and may have a different experience or point of view based on that system and its values. However, it may be difficult for Charles to understand the values of a different system. Responsibility, respect, and integrity are important values for him. Maintaining the social system and its legal rights has high priority. Yet he may stereotype different social systems. Here is how he might think about the same issues:

- Gays and lesbians should be ordained, because any homosexual in ministry who has struggled with the problem of "coming out" in an institution that may not practice mercy and justice — his or her integrity could be stronger than that of others who have not so struggled.

- Gays and lesbians should not be ordained, because this goes against church polity. As a minister I would vote against it, even though it means going against my conscience.

- Liberals [or fundamentalists] can be respected, because, even if mistaken, they have the good of society in mind.

- Liberals [or fundamentalists] should not be tolerated, because their ideas and values are disruptive to society.

Dialectical Donna takes the role of other persons and their social systems and worldviews in all of their complexity. She sees others as persons of intrinsic worth. In her role-taking ability, she considers basic rights, which underlie and can supersede societal and legal rights. Her thinking about these issues can become rather complex, as these examples illustrate:

- In regard to the ordination of gays and lesbians, we need to start from the assumption that as individuals, they are as diverse as heterosexuals; also, that the church is struggling with a variety of interpretations of scripture. Gays and lesbians should not be used as pawns in this struggle but should be treated as persons of intrinsic worth. In making a decision, we must be sure we are using responsible methods of biblical interpretation and are looking at the intrinsic worth of each person.

- Liberalism [or fundamentalism] is a diverse value system that includes individuals with differing responses to it. To judge and treat any individual on the basis of stereotypes is to treat that person as an object rather than as a human being of intrinsic value. Any response needs to be in the spirit of preserving the dignity of the other, while at the same time not tolerating the abuse of any basic rights.

Understanding Perspectives Other Than One's Own

Each perspective has its own distinctive way of role-taking. We offer the following suggestions about each's understanding of the other perspectives.[3]

Dialectical Donna has the capacity to empathize with the other perspectives. Nevertheless, that ability may lead to her frustration and isolation. For example, she may understand the absolutist reasoning of perspective A and the multiplistic thinking of perspective B but still find it very difficult to communicate her understanding of authority that is partial and dialectical to these perspectives.

Conceptualizing Charles has the rational capacity to understand each of the other perspectives but can be limited by that same capacity. For example, Charles might be able to hear Affiliating Al's claims for absolutes and Bargaining Betty's assertion of her own preferences but discount both for their naïveté. Or Charles might find it difficult to understand Al and Betty because of his own embeddedness in rational structures. Charles may reason analytically with Donna but conclude that her notions of truth are inconsistent.

Bargaining Betty might resonate with what she can understand about the relativistic thinking of Charles, because it seems to honor the diversity that she finds. Betty may understand Al's truth and authority claims but disagree with them on the basis of her own preferences. She may prefer but not be able to emulate Donna's way of thinking about the intrinsic worth of each person, the weighing of different sources of authority, or the sense that one's commitment to truth might change.

Affiliating Al may appreciate the tone of Donna's feeling but may think that Charles is cold and Betty is too subjective. Hence, it could be extremely difficult for him to take the role of persons who situate themselves outside of a perspective A circle of absolutes, external authorities, and shared values. Yet Al may also be able to express profound concern and sympathy for persons representing other perspectives, especially if those "others" are experiencing pain and hardship.

Nurturing Empathy

Dialogue that exposes us to other perspectives of faith or ways of thinking not only increases our understanding of others; it also helps us see options

---

3. These descriptions are adapted from H. Edward Everding Jr. and Lucinda A. Huffaker, "Educating Adults for Empathy: Implications of Cognitive Role-Taking and Identity Formation," *Religious Education* (in press).

that become our own seeds of change. Taking this seriously, we can begin to ponder what each perspective might contribute to the empathic ability of the other perspectives. That is, how can one perspective enhance the role-taking abilities of the other perspectives? Or, how does Bargaining Betty function in the community so as to nurture or enhance the empathic ability of Conceptualizing Charles? These "gifts" to the community may function completely unconsciously! For example, Affiliating Al could challenge Bargaining Betty to articulate her feelings about issues and perhaps to justify her subjective approach. Al's perspective can be a reminder to Conceptualizing Charles of the importance of feelings in addition to rationality. Al can also request that Charles explain why there are no absolutes, or why an institution is more important than an individual, or why one should analyze everything. Al can challenge Dialectical Donna to reconsider her understanding of commitment and to affirm the quality of Al's interpersonal relationships.

Bargaining Betty may challenge Al by helping him to see diversity and multiplicity as a fact of life. Betty will emphasize the value of tolerance while understanding Al's insistence on absolute truths. Betty can look to Charles to help her think things out. She has gut feelings about issues, but she can learn from Charles's perspective to develop criteria and a rational argument to express those gut feelings without being labeled "simplistic." Through Betty's valuing of multiplicity, Donna can be stimulated to keep alive the dialectic of her own integrative process of thinking.

Conceptualizing Charles might confront Al and Betty with questions about developing criteria, exploring the vicissitudes of logic, the importance of societal dimensions of human existence, or institutional loyalties. Charles might challenge Donna to articulate the universal principles to which she is committed.

Dialectical Donna has the capacity to take the role of each of the other perspectives. In so doing, she can affirm their individual ways of thinking, regardless of any alleged limitations they may have. Donna could seek to broaden the scope of the distinctive mode of reasoning represented by each perspective, for example, by affirming truth in all of its diversity for Al, affirming tolerance of diversity while raising issues of limits and boundaries for Betty, affirming the rational construction and maintenance of systems for Charles, and insisting on the intrinsic worth of each person.

Nurturing adults' faith perspectives for empathy involves offering various opportunities for enriching their experience and understanding of others in contexts where difference is not experienced as a threat to one's self-expression. These opportunities include forms of play, practice in listening, the offer of options of different faith perspectives, and the exploration of new paradigms of reality and thought, especially within communal learning situations in which the various faith perspectives can interact.[4]

---

4. These strategies are described in ibid.

Learning communities can have a limiting or expanding influence on persons' development of the capacity for empathy. A modal level of a learning community's faith perspective (e.g., perspective A) can act as a ceiling for the practice of role-taking, for example, by setting rigid boundaries around one's interactions with others who think differently. Other modal levels can greatly open up that practice. Conversely, persons' capacities for empathy contribute to the formation and nurture of a learning community's modal level of faith perspective.

Nurturing Faith Perspectives on Empathy through Simulation

The following simulation was developed to help participants explore the issue of the ordination of homosexuals. It involves the participants in both biblical interpretation and role-taking of the four adult perspectives of interpretation.

There are two main purposes for the simulation. First, it gives participants an opportunity to take the role of a faith perspective and to enact that role in a decision-making situation. For purposes of the simulation, each perspective is represented by two groups, because each can develop at least one pro and one con position (other positions might include abstaining or suggesting alternatives to the committee's process). Second, the simulation provides participants with the experience of hearing and relating to these different ways of thinking as they interact with other perspectives. It helps them acknowledge both the difficulties of communication and the opportunities for creative approaches to understanding.

Instructions and Tasks

Divide the participants into eight groups, and distribute to each group the following instructions and one set of tasks identified by a title such as "Group 1: Perspective A." Allow sufficient time for preparation and debriefing.

INSTRUCTIONS:

1. You are members of a conference called to reconsider your denomination's polity, which currently excludes homosexuals from ordination to ministry.

2. In a small group, you will prepare for this conference by taking the role of one of the adult perspectives of faith (A, B, C, or D). From this perspective, you will interpret one biblical text that is usually cited in such discussions and determine how it relates to issues of truth and justice. Each group will have thirty minutes to prepare for the conference.

3. Based on your perspective's reasoning, you will prepare arguments for either a pro or a con response to the question "Should our denomination retain its policy to exclude homosexuals from ordination to ministry?"

4. You should *not* disclose the perspective you are representing during the conference's deliberations.

5. The leader will convene the conference, which will proceed in the following way:

   a. Each perspective will be given two minutes to present its position and arguments.

   b. Each perspective will be allowed two one-minute responses to any of the other positions and arguments presented.

   c. Prior to the vote by the conference, each group will meet for five minutes to prepare for the vote. *Each* member of the group will have one vote and is free to vote either pro or con to the question, based on the reasoning of the perspective for which the group took the role.

   d. The leader will reconvene the conference and call for the vote.

6. After the vote, participants will be asked to break from their roles in order to debrief and evaluate the simulation for twenty to thirty minutes.

Although the leader distributes an individual set of tasks for each group, to eliminate repetition we will list here the common tasks for each perspective and note only the different positions for each group within the same perspective.

GROUPS 1 AND 2: PERSPECTIVE A

Text: Genesis 19:1–11 and God's promise to Abraham (see Gen. 18:22–33)

1. After reading the text aloud, share what was offensive in this story.

2. What was the intended behavior of the "men of Sodom"?

3. What do you think was the purpose of that behavior?

4. What was the sin of Sodom for which "the outcry against its people has become great before the Lord" (19:13 NRSV)? See how that sin was understood in other texts, for example, Isaiah 1:4, 7–10; Jeremiah 23:14; Ezekiel 16:48–49; Matthew 10:14–15; Luke 10:10–12; 2 Peter 2:4–11; and Jude 5–7.

Truth is absolute and abstract. It's right or wrong. It is derived from external authority and unexamined. Justice, or what is right, is interpreted in terms of conformity to conventional images of virtuous behavior. Good intentions, "correct" feelings, and doing good are some of the virtues that indicate what is right.

- *Position for Group 1: Perspective A:* Gays and lesbians should not be ordained, because they are an "abomination" in the eyes of the Bible and are generally disapproved of by most people.

- *Position for Group 2: Perspective A:* Gays and lesbians should be ordained if they are well-intentioned and can perform a caring ministry.

GROUPS 3 AND 4: PERSPECTIVE B

Text: Leviticus 18:22 and 20:13

1. What does the text say?

2. To whom is the law addressed?

3. What kind of behavior is indicated and prohibited? What reason or reasons are given for this behavior to be labeled "an abomination"?

4. The "holiness laws" in Leviticus 17–26 deal with lists of "unmixable" classes or categories. Note the introductions to various lists in 17:1; 18:1–5; 19:1–2; 20:1 and so forth. What were the purposes of these lists for Israel?

5. What other behaviors are listed in the immediate context of 18:22 and 20:13? Are the prohibited behaviors similar or different? What do you think was the purpose of listing these kinds of behaviors?

Truth is whatever each person feels is true. Truth can be different for different people (until it interferes with "my" truth). The only criterion for deciding among competing truth claims is "what feels right." Truth is derived from external authority. Absolute truth is "out there" somewhere, but we can't always find out what it is. Justice, or what is right, is interpreted in terms of conventional images of virtuous behavior. However, latitude is given to persons who do not conform, if they feel that they are doing what is right, have good intentions, and do not impose their behavior on others who do not approve of them.

- *Position for Group 3: Perspective B:* Gays and lesbians should not be ordained, because they will impose their lifestyle on our young people and alienate church members.

- *Position for Group 4: Perspective B:* Gays and lesbians should be ordained, because they feel that they are called by God to minister just as anyone else feels that she or he is called by God to minister.... I guess I don't see sexual preference as interfering with ministry.

GROUPS 5 AND 6: PERSPECTIVE C

Text: Romans 1:26–27

1. What kind of behavior is attributed to "their women" and "the men"?

2. When Paul refers to "them" (1:26), he refers to Greeks or Gentiles. Here it is necessary to read for the context, beginning at 1:16. In 1:16–17, Paul states the letter's thesis about God's salvation and righteousness. Beginning at 1:18, Paul presents an extensive discussion about the "wrath of God" for gentile sin (1:18–32) and Jewish sin (2:1–3:8) and concludes that "all, both Jews and Greeks, are under the power of sin" (3:9), which is elaborated in 3:9–20. This constitutes his long prelude to a lengthy discussion in 3:21–8:39 about God's righteousness and salvation "for all who believe" (3:22).

3. What is "this reason" why "God gave them up to degrading passions"? (See 1:18–25 for Paul's discussion of the "sin" or "error.")

4. Are the "unnatural" sexual relationships the only result of this sin? (See 1:28–32.)

5. How does Paul characterize or describe the unnatural relations in 1:26–27? Why do you think he referred to these as not "natural"?

6. What do you think was Paul's purpose in emphasizing that "God gave them up" (1:24, 26, 28) to these various behaviors?

Truth is viewed in terms of what is "valid" rather than what is "true." Validity is determined by the use of analysis, rational criteria, and consistency. Truth claims are assessed according to a rational relativism and are dichotomized into either/or choices based upon their relative validity. Authority for determining validity is internalized. Justice, or what is right, is understood in terms of the maintenance of "our" systems and their values, responsibility to a given system (e.g., church, society), and contributions to society or an institution. Basic rights are considered important.

- *Position for Group 5: Perspective C:* Gays and lesbians should not be ordained, because, even if they are well-intentioned, they will disrupt the institution just by their presence. Their contribution to the church will always be questioned by a large number of persons, and thus the institution will be jeopardized.

- *Position for Group 6: Perspective C:* Gays and lesbians should be ordained, because they make significant contributions to the maintenance and growth of the church. They provide a prophetic voice for the church that celebrates diversity. . . . It is important to treat each person with respect.

GROUPS 7 AND 8: PERSPECTIVE D

Text: 1 Corinthians 6:9–11

1. The word *homosexuals* first appeared in the Bible with the 1946 RSV translation of this text. Contrast how these verses are translated in the RSV (1972), NEB, JB, and TEV. Then compare the translations in table 14, including a translation by Edgar Goodspeed.[5] The translations differ because the translators were seeking to identify Paul's intended meaning of two Greek words: *malakoi* and *arsenokoitai*. The former meant "soft," with derivative meanings of "effeminate" or "passive," or a male who plays the part of a female, hence "catamite." The latter was a compound word comprising "male" and "bed" and had the connotation of a male who lies with a male, hence "sodomite." This is the earliest known occurrence of *arsenokoitai* in all of Greek literature.

2. What other behaviors are listed in 6:9–10? What was Paul's conclusion in 6:11?

3. What was Paul's purpose for this list and its conclusion in relation to his discussion in 6:1–8? in relation to his discussion in 6:12–20?

Truth is rooted in history and community and is that to which one is committed at a particular moment in life. It has been consciously chosen and integrated from among many choices and by the use of different criteria. Commitment is made in the expectation that it may change and grow. Authority is internalized, yet external sources of authority should be considered and weighed in a dialectical process. Justice, or what is right, is perceived in terms of universal principles that undergird, inform, and transcend systems. Justice is viewed as equality of basic rights and consideration of all persons as of equal worth. Justice is determined by balancing moral and legal points of view.

- *Position of Group 7: Perspective D:* The ordination of gays and lesbians is a difficult matter, because one needs to assess basic rights of all persons, including those who agree and those who do not agree with their ordination. The conflict that results may best be served by developing polity that starts with some sort of compromise, as limiting as that may be to all persons involved. When people are treated justly, they may become more open to treating others with justice.

---

5. Edgar J. Goodspeed, *The New Testament: An American Translation* (Chicago: University of Chicago Press, 1948). This is Goodspeed's modern-speech version of the New Testament.

Table 14
Various Translations of 1 Corinthians 6:9–11

KJV	RSV (1946)	RSV (1972)	NRSV (1989)	Goodspeed
Know ye not that the un-righteous shall not inherit the king-dom of God? Be not de-ceived: neither fornicators (*pornoi*), nor idolaters, nor adulterers, nor **effeminate** (*malakoi*), nor **abusers of themselves with mankind** (*arsenokoitai*), nor thieves, nor covetous, nor drunkards, nor revilers, nor extor-tioners, shall inherit the kingdom of God. And such were some of you: but ye are washed, but ye are sanc-tified, but ye are justified in the name of the Lord Jesus, and by the Spirit of our God.	Do you not know that the unrighteous will not inherit the kingdom of God? Do not be de-ceived; neither the immoral (*pornoi*), nor idolaters, nor adulterers, nor **homosexuals** (*malakoi* and *arsenokoitai*), nor thieves, nor the greedy, nor drunkards, nor revilers, nor robbers will inherit the kingdom of God. And such were some of you. But you were washed, you were sanc-tified, you were justified in the name of the Lord Jesus Christ and in the Spirit of our God.	neither the immoral (*pornoi*), nor idolaters, nor adulterers, nor **sexual perverts** (*malakoi* and *arsenokoitai*), nor thieves,	Fornicators, (*pornoi*), idolaters, adul-terers, **male prostitutes** (*malakoi*), **sodomites** (*ar-senokoitai*), thieves,	People who are immoral (*pornoi*) or idolaters or adulterers or **sensual** (*malakoi*) or **given to un-natural vice** (*arsenokoitai*)

- *Position of Group 8: Perspective D:* Because all persons are of equal worth, it would be unjust to discriminate against anyone just because they were born black, white, female, male, gay, lesbian, straight, and so forth. It is appropriate to develop criteria for ministry that do not include such prejudices and by which all persons would be evaluated equally. When one begins to classify people as black or white, or in any such way, it really violates their rights and basic justice.

Debriefing and Reflections

We reiterate the importance of having sufficient time (at least thirty minutes) to debrief the simulation. Feelings can become very strong, as is indicated by one actual participant's comment that she did not "feel the love of God in the room." Many will enjoy the experience, because it helps them get an idea of the diversity generated by perspectives in addition to opinions, even though they may be uncomfortable with that diversity. It raises for some the question how to affirm and relate to those who represent very different ways of thinking.

Actual participants have identified some of the following as important insights for them about the function of faith perspectives for empathy and in decision-making situations:

1. It is difficult to reason with persons representing quite different ways of thinking, and it takes much energy and skill.

2. Some participants found it easier to affirm persons reasoning out of the same perspective. For example, groups 1 and 2 using A reasoning (pro or con) tended to dismiss other perspectives as irrelevant.

3. The experience reminded participants to prepare carefully their biblical interpretations, especially when relating to persons who may use the Bible in an absolutist and stereotypical way.

4. To change other persons' ways of thinking, let alone one's own, requires a long-term process. Nevertheless, the exchange of ways of thinking is a process through which persons can educate each other, and seeing other options is a necessary precursor to that long-term process of change.

5. Ground rules are necessary to facilitate hearing each other's perspectives, for example, limiting the number of times to speak and the amount of time for each speaker, and treating each speaker's position with respect.

6. Perspective D participants have difficulty being "heard." And perspective A and B participants consider perspective C participants to be too cold or detached.

7. Few persons are able to enter dialogue such as this with the idea that they will be changed.

Conclusion

As some of the preceding observations suggest, practicing and developing empathy can be a very risky business. Nurturing for empathy requires an environment that enhances a person's receptive posture toward others and encourages a degree of self-understanding and ownership of one's emotional investments. Differences in persons' abilities to take the role of others help explain some of the more difficult obstacles to mutual understanding. Even so, an understanding of faith perspectives offers hope for our ability to challenge and enhance one another's growth in empathy, keeping in mind that supportive environments are an essential ingredient for that dynamic process to take place.

12

NURTURING FAITH PERSPECTIVES ON WORSHIP

I will pray with the spirit, but I will pray with the mind also; I will sing praise with the spirit, but I will sing praise with the mind also.
— 1 Corinthians 14:15 NRSV

A worship service that engages its participants only cognitively would be a rather dull and limited religious experience. As a dynamic process, faith gains fullest embodiment through a variety of expressions. In addition to one's cognitive perspectives, expressions of faith can be observed in one's volition, emotion, sensation, action, imagination, and intuition. However, cognitive processes, because they are accessed through language, are the predominant means for interpreting and communicating faith's other expressions. Hence, faith perspectives supply a distinctive coordinating and meaning-making function. As soon as we begin to talk about our religious experience, we are thinking about it within the framework of a perspective of faith. At the same time, interpreting any aspect of a religious experience through any one of the perspectives of faith also limits the full dynamics of that experience. The fullness of experience is inevitably diminished as it is reduced to words.[1]

The apostle Paul understood the interconnections between experiences of prayer and singing "with the mind" and "with the spirit." However, in the context of the Corinthian controversy, he emphasized the relative importance of cognitive instruction within the gathered community: "Nevertheless, in church I would rather speak five words with my mind, in order to instruct others also, than ten thousand words in a tongue" (1 Cor. 14:19 NRSV).

---

1. An excellent analysis of the distinction between description and explanation of religious experience is presented by Wayne Proudfoot, *Religious Experience* (Berkeley: University of California Press, 1985).

If we keep in mind that our thinking and talking about a worship experience cannot contain its fullness, then we are better able to recognize that our knowing is partial. We can begin to appreciate the different ways that people express their faith in worship.

Faith Perspectives on Prayer

Perspectives of faith help us understand persons' experiences of praying with the spirit, experiences that are both real and profound. When we talk with one another about prayer, we organize and communicate our thoughts by means of faith perspectives. For example, Affiliating Al understands his experience of prayer as a personal relationship with God or with Jesus. In his praying, he speaks to God personally as to a friend and a loving parent or as to a judge and a punishing parent. He may feel confirmed if God hears and answers his prayer. He may feel discouraged and abandoned if God never hears or answers his prayer. He has difficulty adjudicating such possibly conflicting experiences of prayer.

Bargaining Betty thinks prayer is whatever she feels is her personal way of relating to God or to whomever she speaks in prayer. She does not necessarily make bargains with God, but she feels that others can have different ideas about prayer, as long as they do not expect her to embrace them. Be and let be is the bargain. Like Al, Betty also has difficulty resolving the tension between answered and unanswered prayer. Her own subjective and personal relationship with God can be strengthened or diminished, depending on how she understands God's response to her.

For Conceptualizing Charles, prayer is the individual or corporate expression of ultimate concern about issues, situations, and persons. His abstract concepts of God may lead him to express ultimate concerns, for example, about social justice or human liberation or global survival. He may not pray personally to God per se but rather may lift up these concerns for himself or for a worshiping community as having universal importance. He may also entrust his concerns to a universal life force that he believes is evolving toward a more ordered complexity. If his concerns are not realized, then his confidence may be shaken by what might appear to be reversals of his expectations.

Dialectical Donna believes that prayer connects individuals to one another and to God in personal, mystical, and universal interdependence. For her, God is an all-encompassing reality, that power of love in which the universe resides and has its being. She prays with all her heart, mind, soul, and strength to God as both a living presence and a universal force for wholeness. Yet she is aware that there is always more to God than she can understand. So she opens herself to the dialectical realities of both disappointment and hope.

Faith Perspectives and Corporate Worship

Worship committees often deliberate about the meaning and structure of worship services. They are aware that persons have different opinions about worship and a variety of ways of expressing those opinions. Adult faith perspectives contribute to this diversity. Understanding how and why faith perspectives shape persons' interpretations of worship may enhance communication and the process of educating adults about their congregation's or denomination's understandings and practices of worship. The distinctive features of each perspective can be illustrated in their respective understandings of proper worship and the Eucharist, or Lord's Supper.

Affiliating Al feels that proper worship is what one has been taught and where one finds meaning and good feelings. Changing worship is the same as changing reality or moving the furniture in heaven. In a worship service, the offering always comes before the sermon. The Lord's Supper is the sacrament in which the church celebrates its common beliefs and values or in which each individual comes to God personally for forgiveness. In Al's church, it is always "done" at the altar rail with individual cups.

Bargaining Betty thinks that proper worship is what one feels it should be. One person's idea is just as good as anyone else's. Does it really matter where the offering comes in the service? She feels that the Lord's Supper can mean different things to different people. It doesn't matter whether one feels that it is a community thing or an individual thing, just as long as everyone can celebrate it in a personally meaningful way. It also doesn't matter whether it is "done" at the altar or in the pew; it's how each one feels about it that counts.

Conceptualizing Charles reasons that proper worship can take many forms, as long as it is consistent with church standards, and it needs evaluation for such consistency (if it is known that such standards exist). Because the offering is the congregation's response to the word of God in scripture and sermon, it must come after the sermon. Charles reasons that the "real" meaning of the Lord's Supper consists in what the symbols of bread and wine signify. They may represent Christ's life-giving sacrifice and the continuing life in Christ of all true believers. The table, then, may be opened only to those who are baptized Christians; it depends on the polity of the congregation or denomination.

Dialectical Donna believes that proper worship provides a confluence of experiences so that persons are able to participate through thinking, imagining, feeling, and doing from whatever perspective they bring to ritual and symbol. Wherever the community decides to locate the offering, it should be at a time when the congregation expresses its love of God and humanity with all its heart, mind, and soul. Donna believes that the Lord's Supper dramatizes the "scandal of particularity," in that God's love expressed in Christ's sacrificial life is for the liberation and transformation of all persons and all reality. The symbol invites all persons to participate in the living presence of the mystical Christ, in whom all things cohere.

Given these representative descriptions, we can understand why cherished symbols related to worship often occasion strong interplay among the faith perspectives. In *The Parable of Ten Preachers*, Thomas H. Troeger has the fictional homiletics professor Peter Linden recall a preaching class attended by ten very different students.[2] Among these is Jason Kirk, a sixty-six-year-old pastor of Clydes Corners, who recounted the battle in his rural church over "the red horsehair couch in our chancel." The couch, placed in "the raised chancel behind the pulpit," had been donated by the founder of Clydes Corners, Cedric Clyde, to show his thanks to God. What a couch!

> The hulking object featured massive curved arms and dark mahogany legs, carved like the claw of a lion. If any strangers who knew nothing about the faith had entered the sanctuary, they would have concluded that the central religious symbol of Christianity was not the small brass cross on the table but the humongous couch in the chancel.

The Clydes, depicting perspective A, understood that couch as a symbol of their great-grandfather Cedric and as what the house of prayer should be with the preacher sitting on it. Newer members, also representing perspective A, saw it as "the Victorian Leviathan," a countersymbol of simpler values they hoped to find in the countryside. These perspectives were at war. Jason, representing perspective C, was conceptualizing about the love of God and, in his own thinking, trying to find reasons to get rid of the couch. Yet he was aware that as he preached, everything he said was filtered through a single question: "Is the pastor in favor of the red horsehair couch, or is the pastor against the red horsehair couch?"

In Troeger's fictional episode, we see perspectives "at war." The couch and its symbolized meanings of affection for Cedric Clyde and what he stood for are emotionally bonded and embedded for the warring factions representing perspective A (in this case both negatively and positively). Understanding their ways of interpreting religious experience might have given preacher Jason some clues for discovering a win/win situation. But he didn't. However, he at least learned that his Conceptualizing Charles style of preaching about a "high and mighty God" was ineffective. His "emotional honesty" opened him to a perspective D view that "faith ranges far beyond what any of us had ever imagined."[3]

This "parable of the red horsehair couch" represents the challenge for congregations to provide opportunities for persons to express their different perspectives of faith about worship and symbols of worship within a safe

---

2. Thomas H. Troeger, *The Parable of Ten Preachers* (Nashville: Abingdon, 1992), 20ff.
3. Ibid., 23, 68, 69.

environment that makes allowances for those differences and offers ways for seeking common ground.

Faith Perspectives and Preaching

What are some implications of the perspectives of faith for preaching? How might the preacher utilize this typology to communicate to persons who "construct" sermons through their distinctive ways of hearing and interpreting?[4] How can a pastor develop the art of perspectival preaching about the religious symbols that generate and regenerate faith?

Pastors who are aware of adult perspectives of interpretation should be *intentional* in both their choice of symbols and their own mode of interpreting the symbols in a sermon. If a sermon centers solely on interpersonal symbols and understandings of the Bible or God (i.e., perspectives A or B), then the sermon may not engage the critical or integrating forms of understanding represented by perspectives C and D. Likewise, if a sermon seeks to explicate an understanding of God as an all-encompassing reality (perspective D), it may be heard as "God is my friend" (perspectives A and B), or it could be dismissed as idealistic imprecision (perspective C). The challenge is to choose carefully content and forms of expression to communicate a vision of a symbol to persons with different perspectives.

A symbol can be shared in such a way that it communicates to persons representing different perspectives of faith by incorporating two or more possible interpretations. Since perspectives A, B, and C represent the modal levels of interpretation in most congregations, the pastor should be sure that these perspectives are included. Using anecdotes and discursive explanations, a sermon can build on the concrete symbol in a spiraling effect, adding layers of meaning. Preachers would be well advised not to preach in a "monotone" of one perspective of interpretation!

Considering story as symbol may help the pastor to be conscious of multiple layers of meaning of religious symbols and to be excited when persons discover their own meanings of a story in relation to those of the sermon. Jesus must have been aware of the communication potential in his use of parables. A parable has the capacity of being understood as a moral example (perspectives A and B) or allegory (all perspectives) or paradox and metaphor (perspectives C and D). Hence, in a sermon, one might make use of a story being aware of all of these potential meanings. For example, persons may understand the parable of the lost sheep (Luke 15:1–7) as an example of caring for the homeless and/or an allegory of God's love for the outcasts of the world and/or a metaphor in which the action of repentance

---

4. Richard F. Ward describes how persons actively "construct" sermons out of what they hear the preacher say. See his "The Listener as Active Participant," in *Speaking from the Heart: Preaching with Passion* (Nashville: Abingdon, 1992), 109–28.

is the experience of being found and/or a paradox of the carelessness of godly caring. Giving some thought to the variety of perspectives represented in the congregation, perhaps even constructing a perspectival interpretation grid of key images or points, will enhance a preacher's communication of the sermon's message.

Perspectives of Faith and Singing with the Spirit

We sing "with the spirit," to be sure. We also sing "with the mind." Singing generates feelings, memories, images, and ideas, all of which are filtered through one's perspective of faith. When persons who have used the old Methodist hymnal sing or hear "Holy, holy, holy! Lord God Almighty!" they might associate feelings and memories with their experiences of the Lord's Supper, because that hymn was an integral part of the Methodist Communion service. And they will also talk about those experiences from the particular perspective of faith that shapes their interpretation. They may sing that hymn "with the spirit," and they will also understand it "with the mind."

The pastor or the worship committee can use perspectival theory to evaluate what perspective(s) the words of a hymn might project or how they might be understood. In addition to their content, hymns, therefore, can be selected to contribute to the perspectives being expressed throughout the worship service. If the purpose of a service is to reinforce a congregation's understanding of itself as an institution (i.e., perspective C), then a hymn such as "The Church's One Foundation" would be appropriate, because it emphasizes the basis of the institution as "one foundation" in its confession of faith and its election "from every nation."

We have noticed that many hymns contain elements that we have come to associate with perspectives A and B. However, any hymn, regardless of the perspective it might suggest, could be interpreted differently by each one of the perspectives. "In the Garden" could represent an expression of Affiliating Al's interpersonal world (e.g., "And he walks with me, and he talks with me"). Conceptualizing Charles might discount the hymn because of its interpersonal sentimentality, or he might appropriate clauses such as "his voice to me is calling" as expressions of a person's covenantal relation with God. Dialectical Donna might let the personal feelings attached to the hymn from memories of earlier times float back into a developing vision of the interdependence of all life in a universal garden or paradise.[5] Hymns can be intentionally chosen to appeal to certain perspectives and/or to provide stimulation to think new thoughts and imagine new symbols of the faith.

---

5. A woman representing "constructed knowledge" refers to this way of thinking as letting the "pieces of myself float back in," in Belenky et al., *Women's Ways of Knowing*, 132.

Nurturing Faith Perspectives on Worship through Role-Play

The worship committee offers a unique opportunity for nurturing faith perspectives on worship. In the process of creating worship experiences and conversing about the meanings of worship, different perspectives can be expressed with integrity and heard with respect. A committee environment of "speaking the truth in love" (Ephesians 4:15) honors the integrity of each perspective despite the differences of opinions and ways of expressing those opinions.

Sometimes "speaking the truth in love" can become uncomfortable because of the different values that persons cherish, as well as the different ways they think about their values. Debates about new books of common prayer or hymnals or inclusive language translations of the Bible often reflect the different perspectives' ways of making sense of the values that people hold. Affiliating Al feels that values are absolute, fixed truths that clearly demarcate right and wrong. Conflicts among one's own values are often not perceived. Bargaining Betty thinks that everyone's values are equally important. Conceptualizing Charles reasons that values are complex and need to be critically evaluated for consistency and rationality. Charles tends to raise more questions about values than he provides answers. Dialectical Donna believes that values are rooted in history and community. They are understood as universal principles and are chosen through a dialectical process of assessing traditional authorities. Donna asserts that values are worthy of commitment even though they might change.

Role-playing can help persons hear different opinions and perspectives while diffusing some of the intense feelings that accompany those differences. Before engaging in debate about an issue such as using contemporary forms of worship or choosing a different hymnal, a worship committee can role-play a decision-making situation using the four perspectives of faith. This will help committee members express and listen to different ways of thinking about the issue. The process may then contribute to better informed and less heated discussions in actual decision-making situations.

The following incident sparked the idea for a role-play dealing with the Lord's Supper. A large family gathering at Easter included participation in a festival Eucharist at a local Episcopal cathedral. Instructions for Communion at this service were printed in the service leaflet:

ALL BAPTIZED CHRISTIANS ARE WELCOME TO RECEIVE COMMUNION: At the direction of the usher, move to the altar rail or to one of the Communion stations. To receive the consecrated bread, extend your hands upward, palms crossed. When receiving the wine, please assist the chalice as it is offered. It is the custom in the Episcopal church for children to receive Communion as soon as they are ready.

As the family proceeded to a Communion station, the father's eldest daughter, a thirty-two-year-old mother of two young boys, turned to her father and whispered, "What happened to all the little cups?" In her abbreviated experience in a Methodist church, she was accustomed to taking Communion at an altar rail where square pieces of bread were served along with "little cups" of grape juice. For her, that was the way it was done; that was the right way. That experience precipitated a discussion with her father about the practices and meanings of the Lord's Supper.

The Role-Play Issue

This role-play focuses on experimenting with different ways of experiencing the Lord's Supper. An imaginary congregation has always celebrated Communion by having each person go to the front altar rail and receive pieces of bread and cups of grape juice, but some members of the committee think it would be instructive for the congregation to try other ways of sharing the Communion elements. They have suggested two alternative practices:

1. Distributing loaves of bread and cups of grape juice to the congregation seated in the pews. Individuals would take a piece of bread from a loaf and then offer the loaf to their neighbor. For some members of the committee, this symbolizes Christ's and our servanthood. Being served in the pews would symbolize Christ's sacrifice and our ministry to all persons where they are in the world.

2. Offering wafers and a common chalice (one with wine and one with grape juice) in front of the altar rail. Persons suggesting this practice think that it symbolizes our oneness in Christ.

The role-play is designed to last approximately one hour. It should be part of a complete committee meeting scheduled for at least one and one-half hours. After an opening time for worship and clarification of the purpose and schedule for the entire meeting, the following instructions and resource should be distributed and clarified. After the role-play and debriefing, the committee then might address one or more items on its agenda, keeping in mind the dynamics and insights from the role-play.

Instructions for Worship Committee Role-Play

1. Form four groups. Each group will represent one of the following perspectives:

   - *Perspective A:* Committee members who favor how the Lord's Supper has always been done

   - *Perspective B:* Committee members who favor one or both of the new forms

- *Perspective C:* Pastor who favors one or both of the new forms, and committee members who favor how it's always been done

- *Perspective D:* Committee members who favor all three forms

2. Use the descriptions of the perspectives provided in the section "Faith Perspectives and Corporate Worship" earlier in this chapter for developing each perspective's response to the question "Should we experiment with different ways of experiencing the Lord's Supper?"

3. Preparation:

   a. Choose a worship committee member to preside over the meeting. This person will represent perspective A.

   b. Each group will develop reasons for its response(s) to the question.

   c. Each group will have twenty minutes to prepare how role-players will respond to the question while representing their perspective of reasoning.

Enacting the Role-Play

1. The presider will call the committee meeting to order and identify the question for the meeting: "Should we experiment with different ways of experiencing the Lord's Supper?"

2. Role-players can speak at will.

3. Twenty minutes is allowed for the discussion. No vote will be taken.

Debriefing the Role-Play

1. Twenty minutes is devoted to debriefing led by the chair of the worship committee or someone else designated for that purpose.

2. Questions for debriefing:

   a. Ask each group: How did you feel representing your particular perspective?

   b. Ask each group: How did you feel about the other groups and their reasoning?

   c. Ask the presider: How did you feel presiding over this committee?

   d. Ask all: What did you learn about yourself? about this process?

   e. Ask all: How might we apply what we learned to our discussions and decisions as a worship committee?

Worship and Christian Nurture

Corporate worship provides an important opportunity for the nurturing of individual and congregational faith perspectives. Of course, it is not the only means or setting for nurture. Other settings may provide equally important opportunities to reflect on and discuss our worship experiences. We can nurture faith by exploring, utilizing, experimenting, and exchanging faith perspectives on various contents and experiences of the religious life. In concluding this chapter, we list several ways to engage the perspectives and other expressions of faith in such a reflective process.

1. Talk about one's childhood faith, and rework and weave it into the present.

2. Talk about doubts. Search and express feelings. Discover the personal in biblical accounts and relate it to one's own feelings.

3. Learn to talk about beliefs, developing an adequate vocabulary rather than depending on clichés and reductionist words and phrases.

4. Engage in critical thinking processes. Historical-critical methods of Bible study can help here.

5. Discover images of spiritual maturity that can function as visions or lures.

6. Be exposed to conditions, persons, and values that are quite different from one's own settings, relationships, and values. Discover how the Bible can function in this process.

7. Experience acceptance and challenge within the context of an interdependent community of faith.

13

PERSPECTIVES AND COMMUNITY

...until all of us come to the unity of the faith and of the knowledge of the Son of God, to maturity, to the measure of the full stature of Christ. —Ephesians 4:13 NRSV

Diversity is a part of our everyday experience. As consumers, we thrive on it. From breakfast cereals to presidential elections, diversity reinforces our freedom of self-expression. It is also perplexing, because it is unsettling; it puts us off balance by removing us from the center of our private worlds. It is frightening that not everyone is like us, that there are so many shades of right and wrong, that things we thought we understood are not what they seem, and that reality and truth are relative — depending on one's viewpoint.

As Christians, we are called to value persons as God's creation, to honor their dignity and intrinsic worth. Confronted with diversity that seems to threaten who we are and the things we believe, we struggle to fulfill our calling to respect those who are different and to embrace them in some way that is congruent with our faith, maintaining both the integrity of our lives as Christians and their lives of individual choice and freedom. More than that, we are challenged to become vulnerable to their strangeness — as Israel was exhorted to welcome the stranger with hospitality — as God's gift through which our knowledge of God increases.

In this book, we have talked about diversity as it can be attributed to differences in ways people think about and express their faith. As a dynamic process that is constantly relating important values in our lives to our experiences, faith provides a framework through which we interpret or understand the meaning(s) of those experiences. One of the many expressions of these centers of value is each individual's way of thinking and talking about faith, and we have described four perspectives that adults take when they do so.

Although Christian nurture requires the comprehensive support of a variety of explorations and expressions of faith, one important aspect of nurturing faith involves broadening and enriching our ways of thinking, or perspectives, by bringing them into dialogue with other experiences, ex-

148

pressions, and perspectives of faith. Such interactions have a significant impact on the community where they occur, and the positive or negative outcome is often dependent on the degree to which the community can accept its own heterogeneity. Of course, each perspective of faith acknowledges the existence of diversity but will interpret diversity differently, making cooperative endeavors and shared identity even more complex.

The search for common ground and community within a diverse and individualistic culture of opinions, lifestyles, and affections is a formidable challenge to the church. Traditionally the church has looked to its origins, especially those recorded in the Bible, for clues to the creation of new forms of community in changing life situations. In the preceding chapters, we suggested the contributions and liabilities that each of the four perspectives could bring to the search for common understandings. We'll now conclude our reflections by considering what the Bible and the presence of the four perspectives suggest about the search for common ground and community.

Bible and Community

As a "religion of the book," Christianity constitutes itself upon the authority of the Bible, its canon. Although rich in diversity (i.e., in its textuality), the Bible emerged from and testified to events that created and established the identity and lifestyle of the believing community.[1] In relation to this sacred text, the community tells and retells its common story and shapes the character of its common life.[2]

The creation of community is an ongoing process as the community converses with the many canonical voices. Through its own journey, the community attends both to certain voices that confirm its unity of identity and to different voices that adjust to its changing context. At times it may be the voice of creation or exodus. At other times it might be the voice of royal wisdom, prophetic judgment, or an apocalyptic vision of a new world. It is often an expression of parabolic surprise that subverts the established world through healing or justification or liberation. At times a voice from the margin breaks through and speaks the word that does not fit, upsetting the order that seemed so appropriately fixed. In such instances, the canon functions to transform and re-create community.

The canon in all its variety also provides common ground for interpreters to come together for conversation, as well as to go their separate ways. Although persons and groups differ in their interpretations, there is always the text. The text has staying power. The text invites interpreters and gathers diverse persons around it for conversation. The text creates an

---

1. James A. Sanders, *Canon and Community: A Guide to Canonical Criticism* (Philadelphia: Fortress, 1984), 28.
2. David Rhoads, *The Challenge of Diversity: The Witness of Paul and the Gospels* (Minneapolis: Fortress, 1996).

interpreting community by claiming from diverse interpreters allegiance to what it says. It does the work of forming and transforming the community.

Perspectives and Community

Understanding the character of the different perspectives of faith can contribute to community by enhancing the process of communication. It can provide a sense of comfort to individuals, assuring them that there is legitimacy to their viewpoints while also encouraging them toward greater respect and tolerance for others as subjects rather than objects to be molded into conformity. Nevertheless, just knowing that there are differing perspectives on any subject does not guarantee community. Equally important to how diversity enriches us is how it also exposes the partiality and "limitations of our own way."[3] The blind spots in how we understand persons and issues can be brought to light as an important step toward our growth in self-awareness and a more complete knowledge for our pursuit of justice. Hence, a shared vision that projects the value of diversity within the community promotes both acceptance and humility. Biblical images of showing hospitality to the stranger (e.g., Rom. 12:13; Heb. 13:2) and of the church as a "body" with diverse individual parts (e.g., 1 Cor. 12; Eph. 4) are examples of guiding visions that celebrate the plurality of perspectives as a gift of divine grace.

One way that the interplay between individuality of perspectives and community can be portrayed is by an image of truth as communal and relational. In the Ephesians 4 image of the church as the body of Christ, whatever is true is seen in *relation* to Christ as the head, and whatever is true is confirmed in the *communal* relationship of love (v. 15). Truth, then, is not a matter of getting "right knowledge" or "right interpretation." Truth unfolds as we learn and live together what God's reign is for our time and place. In *To Know as We Are Known*, Parker Palmer develops the concept of communal and relational truth: "Truth is found as we are obedient to a pluralistic reality, as we engage in that patient process of dialogue, consensus seeking, and personal transformation in which all parties subject themselves to the bonds of communal troth."[4] Palmer uses the word *troth* because its Germanic root conveys the covenant of mutual transformation one enters when engaged in "truthful knowing:"

> In truthful knowing the knower becomes co-participant in a community of faithful relationships with other persons and creatures and things, with whatever our knowledge makes known. We find truth

---

3. David Tracy, *The Analogical Imagination: Christian Theology and the Culture of Pluralism* (New York: Crossroad, 1981), 252.
4. Palmer, *To Know as We Are Known*, 68.

by pledging our troth, and knowing becomes a reunion of separated beings whose primary bond is not of logic but of love.[5]

Attentiveness to the distinctive features of the four perspectives of faith contributes to "truthful knowing," especially when accompanied by dialogue that seeks mutual respect and understanding. In the gathered life of the faith community where all viewpoints are given the chance to be expressed and heard, truths are learned and created, tested, lived out, refined, and shared. In this dynamic process of faith's seeking and expressing understanding, we discover ultimately that the quality of our love, not logic, enables us "to know fully," even as we have been "fully known."

---

5. Ibid., 22.

Appendix A

FAITH PERSPECTIVES AND BIBLICAL INTERPRETATION

Subject Area	Al	Betty	Charles	Donna
World	Centered on interpersonal relationships, stereotypes; conforms to values of significant others	Multiplistic; centered on interpersonal relationships, one's preferences for diversity	An explicit, rational system; centered on rationality, concepts, ideologies	A pluralistic, ambiguous, or complex unity; centered on vision, integration, basic rights. Can stand outside a system
Reasoning	Abstract, hypothetical, compartmentalized, not analytical, not clearly separated from feelings	Abstract, hypothetical; imitates analytical process, not clearly separated from feelings. Aware of diversity	Abstract, analytical, reflective, dichotomized. Searches for rationality, consistency, coherence; knows intellectual passion and wonder	Abstract, dialectical, paradoxical; moving toward integration. Has critical self-awareness
Interpreting style	Focuses on the abstract and on true meanings, guidelines, and what is useful	Focuses on abstract messages and guidelines that are personally useful but not necessarily useful for others	Analytical, using abstract concepts of meaning	Analytical, uses abstract concepts of meaning; integrates new meanings with personal commitment
Authority of the Bible	External and absolute; tacit and stereotypical	Located in one's personal feelings or preferences in relating to an external absolute; tacit and multiplistic	Located in the system and/or in truth as logically determined by the individual	Partial, weighing with other traditional authorities in a dialectical process; ultimate, internalized in personal commitment
Tradition	An affectional aggregation; a past historical entity	An affectional aggregation; a past historical entity; diverse, to be questioned	Abstract meanings; historical past connected to present; to be analyzed and evaluated	Integration of past; universal and personal; emotional-rational-aesthetic bonding
Images of the Bible	Multidimensional, uncritically apprehended; having one meaning, such as guidelines and examples	Multidimensional, uncritically apprehended; having different meanings for different people	Abstract concepts of meaning and images	Abstract and personal; personal confrontation with God within the context of community and traditions; subject rather than object
Truth	Absolute, abstract, right or wrong	Whatever one feels is true; a hidden, abstract, external absolute	Ideas "valid" rather than "true," determined by use of analysis, rational criteria, consistency; rational relativism	Examined, rooted in history and community; that to which one is committed today
Self as interpreter	Feels sense of growth and internal change; anticipates struggle with diversity	Attuned to multiplistic world, aware of internal change; accepts diversity	Rational and reflective. Feels self-imposed responsibility for growth and creation of meaning	Dialogues with Bible and others as equal subjects; evaluates and integrates thinking and feeling, personal commitment

Appendix B

THE RESEARCH PROJECT

The research that forms the basis for this book was conducted from 1977 to 1983. It consisted of longitudinal studies of students at the Iliff School of Theology in Denver. Students were interviewed as they entered Iliff in the master's program and/or shortly before they graduated, normally after three to four years of study. Carefully designed interview questions provided information about any changes that might have occurred in the interpretive perspectives of the students during that time, as well as information about factors that might have affected those changes or lack of them.

A research team consisting of ourselves and trained graduate students conducted interviews from 1977 to 1983. After the oral interviews were taped and transcribed, the research team analyzed and scored the interviews. The team validated its results in the early stages through collaboration with Kohlberg's Harvard researchers. The results were thoroughly rechecked in the late 1980s and early 1990s. The statistical results are significant only for this population of subjects — graduate students in a school of theology — but the descriptions and implications seem clearly applicable to adults in many other settings.

As it became clear that a significant number of students interviewed at entrance were not available for the exiting interview, we interviewed other exiting students to obtain a more accurate profile of graduating students. All subjects were chosen by random sampling except for seventeen who volunteered in 1977. Statistical analysis showed no distinction between those volunteers and the random sample, so they have been included in the total.

Comparisons were made (1) between men and women, (2) between those students who took a "faith development" course and those who did not, and (3) between those who were a part of the research team and those who were not. The faith development course introduced students to the interpretive perspective model in depth, and it was taught in a manner that attempted to stimulate critical thinking about the content. The research team, thoroughly exposed to different interpretive perspectives and challenged by the constant need to do critical thinking, was included along with those taking faith development as well as analyzed as a separate group. Members of the research team the first year were given additional interviews unlike those used in the research interviewing and scoring. Harvard researchers scored these additional interviews to ascertain whether the interpretive perspective observed in relation to the familiar dilemmas would also apply to unfamiliar ones. In other words, were those subjects giving memorized answers, or were they using basic structures of interpretation? We found that it was the structures of interpretation that were decisive, not learned responses.

The interview for entering students consisted of three moral dilemmas (Kohlberg's moral judgment interviews 3, 3', and 1) and our Biblical Interview. Exiting students were given the same three moral dilemmas for comparison, the Educational Experience Interview, and the Professional Understanding Interview.

Scoring of the responses to the moral dilemmas was based on the standard scoring guide designed by Kohlberg and his associates at the Center for Moral Development, Harvard University.[1] Data from the moral dilemma interviews were analyzed to assess correlations between the scores of responses to the moral dilemmas (Moral Maturity Scores, or MMSs) and the responses to the other parts of the interviews. The scoring models developed by James Fowler and William Perry were also used.[2] For example, in analyzing the style of reasoning disclosed in the Biblical Interviews, we used charts describing different interpretation styles (or stages) for several categories of understanding (e.g., ways of thinking about logic, symbol, social perspective, and truth), as well as charts describing Perry's theory. Interviews were analyzed without knowledge of the subjects' MMSs, and the numerical scores were then compared with the MMSs. Correlations between this method of scoring the Biblical Interviews and the subjects' MMSs were extremely close, almost always below a 10 percent differential. Correlations between Kohlberg's scores and our perspectives are shown in table B.1. As table B.1 suggests, scores often included material from adjacent perspectives. Individual scores for the 83 subjects who participated in the entering interview ranged from 307 to 466, so among the subjects we found the use of all four perspectives (A, B, C, and D). There was no significant correlation between MMS score and age.

Table B.1
Correlations between Kohlberg's Moral Maturity Scores and Adult Faith Perspectives

Kohlberg's Moral Maturity Score (Approximate)	Faith perspectives
300–325	Perspective A, including some B and/or C
325–375	Perspective A and B and/or C
375–400	Perspective C, with some A and/or B
400–450	Perspective C, with some D
450–500	Perspective C, with considerable D

---

1. Kohlberg et al., *Standard Form Scoring Manual*.
2. Fowler, *Stages of Faith*; Perry, *Forms of Intellectual and Ethical Development*.

In the group of 151 subjects who participated in the exiting interview, the average score was the same for men and women. Individual scores ranged from 323 to 493, again demonstrating the presence of all four perspectives in the reasoning of this group. MMSs on Kohlberg's dilemmas and sample characteristics are summarized in table B.2.

Table B.2
Moral Maturity Scores and Sample Characteristics

Total number of interviews = 252[a]	Female and Male	Female	Male
Total subjects interviewed	179	78	101
Average age at time of first interview[b]	30.8	33.5	28.7
Number of subjects with entering interview	56	27	29
Average age	29.6	33.3	25.8
Average entering score	374.1	377.9	370.2
Number of subjects with both entering and exiting interviews	56	27	29
Average age at entering	28.5[c]	31.9	25.4
Average entering score	371.9	378.9	365.3
Average exiting score	418.2	416.5	419.7
Percentage change in score	+12.4%	+9.9%	+14.9%
Average percentage change (ages 21–29)	+15.4%	—	—
Average percentage change (ages 30–52)	+9.1%	—	—
Number of subjects with exiting interview	151	63	88
Average age[b]	30.7	33.0	29.0
Average exiting score	419.8	419.7	419.9
Number with faith development course	86	34	52
Average age	30.6[a]	—	—
Average exiting score	433.4	—	—
Number without faith development course	65	29	36
Average age	30.8[a]	—	—
Average exiting score	401.8	—	—
Number of research team members	29	13	16
Average age	30.3	—	—
Average score after faith development course	431.7	—	—
Average exiting score	458.5	—	—

Note: Dashes indicate items for which we do not provide statistics. As the numbers of subjects became smaller in some samples, we were concerned about statistical significance.

a As is indicated by these figures, some subjects were interviewed more than once.

b The ages of the subjects are those recorded at the time the subject was first interviewed. For 83 subjects, plus 30 research team subjects, this was at the time of the *entering* interview. By contrast, 66 subjects took only the *exiting* interview, and their age was recorded at that time.

c Averages in this column were obtained by averaging all the individual scores, not the averages of the "Female" and "Male" columns.

Comparison of Moral Maturity Scores
with Biblical Interview Scores

The Biblical Interview was administered to *entering* students after they responded to the three moral dilemmas designed by Kohlberg to determine moral reasoning stages. The interview was designed to evoke reasoning about issues such as symbol, logic, truth, persons, authority, and role-taking.

Scoring of Biblical Interviews

Using charts incorporating stage definitions for logical reasoning, symbol, social perspective, and truth, the research team sought to describe the style of reasoning disclosed in the answers to the interview questions. The evaluation was conducted without knowledge of the subjects' MMSs. After some experimenting, a scoring form was designed to record the evaluations of the styles of interpretation (A, B, C, or D) and the spheres of understanding (symbol, logic, truth, persons, authority, and role-taking) discerned in the subjects' answers to each question.

The scoring of the first six interviews resulted in global evaluations of the styles that matched very closely with the MMSs. Also, it became increasingly clear that Perry's theory of intellectual development was invaluable for assisting in the evaluations. Moreover, data from the interviews helped to complete lacunae in charts utilizing Perry's theory.

The process of evaluation was then refined by using a more comprehensive chart, including seventeen spheres of understanding for perspectival interpretation and refined charts of Perry's theory. The evaluations became more precise. The team designed a scoring system that translated the previous global evaluations into numbers that could be more precisely compared with the MMSs. Again, the evaluations were conducted without knowledge of the subjects' MMSs. These scores and their comparisons with the MMS of each subject are listed in table B.3.

Table B.3
Moral Maturity Scores Compared with Biblical Interview Scores

Subjects			Moral Maturity Scores (MMSs)		Percentage Change between Enter/Exit	Biblical Interview Scores (BISs)	Percentage Difference between Entering MMSs and BISs

1977

ID#	Sex	Age	Enter	Exit		Enter	
784	M	22	329	375	+14	343	+4
785	F	32	417	407	-2	398	-5
7823	F	31	370	387	+5	379	+2
7824	F	38	339	389	+15	350	+3
7825	F	25	383	396	+3	405	+6
7828	M	27	365	500	+37	388	+6
7830	M	33	386	431	+12	400	+4
7833	M	22	407	427	+5	402	-1
7838	M	22	313	423	+35	326	+4
7839	M	26	364	496	+36	349	-4
7840	M	27	404	471	+17	392	-3
7843	F	40	337	417	+24	333	-1
7845	M	22	357	369	+3	332	-7
7875	M	29	342	363	+6	336	-2
7877	M	21	307	405	+32	324	+6
7879	M	21	375	392	+5	371	-1
7880	F	23	383	453	+18	369	-4

1978

ID#	Sex	Age	Enter	Exit		Enter	
201	M	32	338	457	+35	346	+2
202	M	24	362	483	+33	385	+6
203	M	23	327	443	+35	328	0
204	M	22	385	397	+3	389	+1
205	M	24	377	400	+6	377	0
206	M	21	350	400	+14	358	+2
207	M	25	373	429	+15	362	-3
208	M	27	407	473	+16	None	--
216	F	22	360	400	+11	354	-2
217	F	23	369	463	+25	364	-1
219	F	22	353	390	+10	329	-7

Table B.3 (continued)
Moral Maturity Scores Compared with Biblical Interview Scores

Subjects			Moral Maturity Scores (MMSs)		Percentage Change between Enter/Exit	Biblical Interview Scores (BISs)	Percentage Difference between Entering MMSs and BISs

1979

ID#	Sex	Age	Enter	Exit		Enter	
7920	F	35	332	376	+13	376	+13
7922	F	22	354	393	+11	334	-6
7926	F	43	304	332	+9	294	-3
7930	M	23	400	433	+8	407	+2
7932	M	46	370	376	+2	389	+5
7933	F	47	367	493	+34	361	-2
7934	F	26	337	365	+8	315	-7
7937	M	23	373	446	+20	366	-2
7938	F	32	407	432	+6	405	0
7939	M	22	368	400	+9	374	+2
7941	F	30	353	380	+8	365	+3
7944	F	52	383	400	+4	375	-2
7945	M	35	383	393	+3	376	-2
7946	M	23	370	400	+8	386	+4
7948	F	41	428	457	+7	395	-8
7950	M	23	354	360	+2	327	-8
7951	M	22	382	450	+18	374	-2
7953	M	30	361	387	+7	342	-5

1980

8010	F	26	408	453	+11	387	-5
8012	F	46	413	446	+8	404	-2
8013	F	40	433	473	+9	433	0
8014	F	22	339	397	+17	332	-2
8015	F	25	396	457	+15	380	-4
8016	F	51	377	400	+6	388	+3
8020	F	23	376	456	+21	375	0
8022	F	32	392	400	+2	406	+4
8024	F	30	450	464	+3	427	-5
8025	F	22	408	473	+16	392	-4

Results

The results of our analysis indicate the use of all four perspectives (A, B, C, and D) in our sample. There was no significant correlation between Kohlberg's Moral Maturity Score and age, although entering women were slightly older and averaged slightly higher in score. Nor was there any significant difference in female and male average scores, which suggests a lack of support in this sample for Carol Gilligan's and others' arguments for a gender bias in Kohlberg's testing instrument.[3]

The increase in the Kohlberg scores in individuals' first (entering) and second (exiting) interviews showed some overall changes in the use of the different interpretive perspectives (see table B.3). Women had a lower percentage of change than did men. We can only speculate that women's older average age (33.5 versus 28.7 for males) was a contributing factor.

Scores for the 151 exiting interviews were almost identical for both men and women. Subjects who had taken "faith development" scored significantly higher than did those who had not been exposed to the theory. Research team members (those who had participated in the scoring process for one year, in a few cases more) scored significantly higher than the average.

It appears that age may affect the average percentage of increase in scores. For ages 21–29, the thirty-six subjects who took both entering and exiting interviews had an average increase of 15.4%, with no decreases. Of those, six (16.7% of the total) had an increase of more than 30%. Of the twenty subjects aged 30–52, the average increase (among eighteen subjects) was 9.1%, with two decreases of 2.4% and .8%. One subject (5% of the total) had an increase of more than 30%. Recognizing that these numbers are not large enough to be statistically significant, the question how age influences change in perspective nevertheless appears to be an important one for further exploration.

The phenomenon that we labeled "encapsulation" appeared in a few interviews where subjects' responses clustered within a single perspective or pair of perspectives. In these interviews, a particular topic would evoke responses markedly different in structure, suggesting that particular content areas were bracketed or encapsulated within a way of thinking much removed from thinking about other areas. These content areas seemed to involve strong emotional investment in such subjects as biblical interpretation or particular religious concepts or secular ideas (e.g., a strongly negative view of authority and the function of law in our society). Encapsulation merits continued investigation to learn more about the interplay of emotion, belief, and critical reflection.

---

3. Carol Gilligan, *In a Different Voice: Psychological Theory and Women's Development* (Cambridge: Harvard University Press, 1982).

Interview Given to Entering Students

Moral Judgment Interview
(prepared by Lawrence Kohlberg)

DILEMMA 3

In Europe, a woman is near death from a special kind of cancer. There is one drug that the doctors think might save her. It is a form of radium that a druggist in the town has recently discovered. The drug was expensive to make, but the druggist is charging ten times what the drug cost him to make. He paid $200 for the radium and is charging $2,000 for a small dose of the drug. The sick woman's husband, Heinz, has gone to everyone he knows to borrow the money, but he has collected only about $1,000, which is half of what the drug costs. He has told the druggist that his wife is dying, and has asked the druggist to sell the drug cheaper or to let him pay later. But the druggist said, "No, I discovered the drug and I'm going to make money from it." Heinz gets desperate and considers breaking into the man's store to steal the drug for his wife.

1. Should Heinz steal the drug? Why or why not?

2. If Heinz doesn't love his wife, should he steal the drug for her? Why or why not?

3. Suppose the person dying is not his wife but a stranger. Should Heinz steal the drug for the stranger? Why or why not?

4. (If you favor Heinz's stealing the drug for a stranger) Suppose it's a pet animal he loves. Should Heinz steal to save the pet animal? Why or why not?

5. Is it important for people to do everything they can to save another's life? Why or why not?

6. It is against the law for Heinz to steal. Does that make it morally wrong? Why or why not?

7. Should people try to do everything they can to obey the law? Why or why not? How does this apply to what Heinz should do?

Major issues: law, life
Secondary issues: affiliation, property, morality, conscience

DILEMMA 3'

Heinz does break into the store. He steals the drug and gives it to his wife. In the newspapers the next day, there is an account of the robbery. Mr. Brown, a police officer who knows Heinz, reads the account. He remembers seeing Heinz running away from the store and realizes that it was Heinz who stole the drug. Mr. Brown wonders whether he should report that Heinz was the robber.

1. Should Officer Brown report Heinz for stealing? Why or why not?

2. Officer Brown finds and arrests Heinz. Heinz is brought to court, and a jury is selected. A jury's job is to find whether a person is innocent or guilty of committing a crime. The jury finds Heinz guilty. It is up to the judge to determine the sentence. Should the judge give Heinz a sentence, or should he suspend the sentence and let Heinz go free? Why?

3. Thinking in terms of society, why should people who break the law be punished? How does this apply to what Heinz should do?

4. Heinz was doing what his conscience told him when he stole the drug. Should a lawbreaker be punished if he is acting out of conscience? Why or why not?

Major issues: morality, conscience, punishment
Secondary issue: life

DILEMMA 1

Joe is a fourteen-year-old boy who wants to go to camp very much. His father promises him he can go if he saves the money for it himself. So Joe works hard at his paper route and saves the $40 it costs to go to camp, and a little more besides. But just before camp is going to start, his father changes his mind. Some of his father's friends have decided to go on a special fishing trip, and Joe's father is short of the money it will cost, so he tells Joe to give him the money Joe has saved from the paper route. Joe doesn't want to give up going to camp, so he thinks of refusing to give his father the money.

1. Should Joe refuse to give his father the money? Why or why not?

2. Is the fact that Joe earned the money himself the most important thing in the situation? Why or why not?

3. The father promised Joe he could go to camp if he earned the money. Is the fact that the father promised the most important thing in the situation? Why or why not?

4. Why, in general, should a promise be kept?

5. Is it important to keep a promise to someone you don't know well and probably won't see again? Why or why not?

6. What do you think is the most important thing a son should be concerned about in his relationship to his father? Why is that the most important thing?

7. What do you think is the most important thing a father should be concerned about in his relationship to his son? Why is that the most important thing?

Major issues: contract, authority
Secondary issues: property, truth, affiliation

Biblical Interview
(prepared by H. Edward Everding Jr.,
Clarence Snelling Jr., and Mary M. Wilcox)

The Pastoral Epistles (1 and 2 Timothy and Titus) contain instructions from the author to persons who are beginning their ministry. The following text may be of interest to those involved in education for ministry.

> But as for you, continue in what you have learned and have firmly believed, knowing from whom you learned it and how from childhood you have been acquainted with the sacred writings which are able to instruct you for salvation through faith in Christ Jesus. All scripture is inspired by God and profitable for teaching, for reproof, for correction, and for training in righteousness, that the man of God may be complete, equipped for every good work. (2 Tim. 3:14–17 RSV)

1. What do you feel stands out for you in this biblical text? Why?

2. What do you think is the main point of the text? What do you think it is all about?

3. What words or phrases help you to see that point?

4. How do you feel about the text? Do you agree or disagree? Why?

5. In light of what you have been saying, would you please summarize what you think the text is all about?

In the text, the writer is instructing Timothy for ministry and refers to others through whom he has learned. You, like Timothy, are being prepared for ministry.

6. What would you expect of an instructor? Why?

7. What would allow you to trust an instructor? Why?

8. What do you think should be the basis for the authority of an instructor? Why?

9. What do you see as most important in the relation between a student and an instructor? Why?

10. If you disagreed with an instructor, what reasons might there be for accepting his or her authority in spite of the disagreement? Why?

In the text, the writer reminds Timothy that from his youth he was acquainted with the sacred writings that now provide the authority for the writer's instructions.

11. What reasons would you give to someone for the authority of the scriptures?

12. What does the phrase "inspired by God" mean to you?

In the text, tradition is described. Timothy learns about the scriptures from significant persons in his childhood. His learning is continued through the writer's example and instruction in the faith. Timothy in turn is then instructed to pass on to others what he has received.

13. What functions as tradition for you? Why?

14. How do you understand yourself in relation to tradition? Why?

15. What is more important to you, the Bible or tradition? Why?

16. When you think of the Bible, what pictures, words, or phrases come to mind?

17. What are your feelings or thoughts about the Bible? Why?

18. What role does the Bible play in your life? Why?

19. Do you feel that your understanding of the Bible is true? Why?

20. Are understandings of the Bible other than your own true? Why?

21. Are there areas in which you wonder or have deep doubts about the Bible? In what sense?

22. What is your understanding of how the Bible came to be?

23. What persons or communities have been most influential in shaping your understanding of the Bible? How?

24. Do you feel that you are changing, growing, struggling in your understanding of the Bible? How?

Issues: authority, truth, sense of historical time, symbol

Interview Given to Exiting Students

Moral Judgment Interviews 3, 3′, and 1

Educational Experience (prepared by Everding, Snelling, and Wilcox)

1. What stands out for you during your Iliff school years? Why? Could you explain that further?

2. Has your thinking changed during your Iliff school years? If so, how and why? What influenced this change?

3. During your lifetime, who or what has most influenced your thinking and values? How?

4. What best helps you to learn a new idea? Why or how do you think that helps you?

5. Do you consider yourself more intuitive/imagistic in your thinking, or more analytical/rational? Can you expand on that?

Professional Understanding (case study prepared by H. Edward Everding Jr. and Dana W. Wilbanks)

You are a member of the board of ministry of a denomination whose polity or law includes the ordination of women. The board is meeting to decide on the ordination of Charles J. It has been determined that, in general, Charles meets the standards of fitness and competence for ministry. However, in discussions with Charles, a major issue has surfaced that raises in the minds of some members of the board an obstacle to his ordination.

Charles has expressed his belief that the church is wrong in ordaining women to the Christian ministry. He believes this practice is contrary to his understanding of the Bible. In response to questions, Charles indicates that he would serve with women who were ordained and he would not seek to prevent the ordination of women, but he could not in conscience vote for the ordination of women or participate in the ordination of women. Some members of the board believe Charles's view so violates the church's understanding of ministry that he should not be ordained.

1. Should the board of ministry ordain Charles? Why or why not?

2. Charles is making his decision out of conscience. Should this fact enter into the decision of the board? Why or why not?

3. Thinking in terms of the church, what would be the best reasons justifying a decision to ordain Charles? not to ordain Charles? Why?

4. What is the purpose or function of church polity or law? Why?

5. In this situation, there is a conflict between the authority of church and civil law, on the one hand, and the authority of biblical interpretation, on the other hand. Where do you think the final authority should lie? Why?

6. What do you think is the most important thing a minister should be concerned about in her or his responsibility to the institutional church?

7. Thinking in terms of society, what would be the best reasons to ordain Charles? not to ordain Charles?

Major issues: law, conscience, authority
Social perspective: community/society/institutions, persons

Bibliography

Anderson, Janice Capel, and Stephen D. Moore, eds. *Mark and Method: New Approaches in Biblical Studies*. Minneapolis: Fortress, 1992.

Anderson, Walter Truett. *Reality Isn't What It Used to Be: Theatrical Politics, Ready-to-Wear Religion, Global Myths, Primitive Chic, and Other Wonders of the Postmodern World*. San Francisco: Harper, 1990.

Astley, Jeff, and Leslie J. Francis, eds. *Christian Perspectives on Faith Development: A Reader*. Grand Rapids, Mich.: Eerdmans, 1992.

Bateson, Mary Catherine. *Composing a Life*. New York: Atlantic Monthly Press, 1989.

Belenky, Mary Field, Blythe McVicker Clinchy, Nancy Rule Goldberger, and Jill Mattuck Tarule. *Women's Ways of Knowing: The Development of Self, Voice, and Mind*. New York: Basic, 1986.

Bellah, Robert, Richard Madsen, William Sullivan, Ann Swindler, and Stephen Tipton. *Habits of the Heart: Individualism and Commitment in American Life*. Berkeley: University of California Press, 1985.

Berger, Peter L., and Thomas Luckman. *The Social Construction of Reality: A Treatise in the Sociology of Knowledge*. Garden City, N.Y.: Doubleday, 1966.

Boys, Mary, ed. *Education for Citizenship and Discipleship*. Cleveland: Pilgrim, 1989.

Brennan, Barbara Ann. *Hands of Light: A Guide to Healing through the Human Energy Field*. New York: Bantam, 1987.

Brueggemann, Walter, Sharon Parks, and Thomas H. Groome. *To Act Justly, Love Tenderly, Walk Humbly: An Agenda for Ministers*. Mahwah, N.J.: Paulist, 1986.

Brunner, Jerome. *Actual Minds, Possible Worlds*. Cambridge: Harvard University Press, 1986.

Bultmann, Rudolf. "The Problem of Hermeneutics." In *Essays: Philosophical and Theological*. New York: Macmillan, 1955.

Bushnell, Horace. *Christian Nurture*. 1861. Reprint, Grand Rapids, Mich.: Baker, 1979, 1984.

Caine, Renate Nummela, and Geoffrey Caine. *Making Connections: Teaching and the Human Brain*. New York: Addison-Wesley, 1994.

Capra, Fritjof. *The Turning Point: Science, Society, and the Rising Culture*. New York: Bantam, 1983.

Chopra, Deepak. *Quantum Healing: Exploring the Frontiers of Mind/Body Medicine*. New York: Bantam, 1989.

Crossan, John Dominic. *In Parables: The Challenge of the Historical Jesus*. New York: Harper & Row, 1973.

————. *Jesus: A Revolutionary Biography.* San Francisco: HarperSanFrancisco, 1994.

Dossey, Larry. *Recovering the Soul: A Scientific and Spiritual Search.* New York: Bantam, 1989.

Dunn, James D. G. *Unity and Diversity in the New Testament: An Inquiry into the Character of Earliest Christianity.* 2d ed. Philadelphia: Trinity, 1990.

Dykstra, Craig. "Faith Development and Religious Education." In *Faith Development and Fowler,* ed. Craig Dykstra and Sharon Parks. Birmingham, Ala.: Religious Education Press, 1986.

Everding, H. Edward, Jr. "A Hermeneutical Approach to Educational Theory." In *Foundations for Christian Education in an Era of Change,* ed. Marvin J. Taylor. Nashville: Abingdon, 1976.

————. "Implications of Jean Piaget's Theory of Cognitive Development for Teaching the Bible: A Programmatic Essay." Paper presented at the annual meeting of the Society of Biblical Literature, Washington, D.C., October 1974.

Everding, H. Edward, Jr., and Lucinda A. Huffaker. "Educating Adults for Empathy: Implications of Cognitive Role-Taking and Identity Formation." *Religious Education,* in press.

Everding, H. Edward, Jr., Clarence H. Snelling Jr., and Mary M. Wilcox. "A Shaping Vision of Community for Teaching in an Individualistic World: Ephesians 4:1–16 and Developmental Interpretation." *Religious Education* 83, no. 3 (summer 1988): 423–37.

————. "Toward a Theory of Instruction for Religious Education." Paper presented at the annual meeting of the Association of Professors and Researchers in Religious Education, Toronto, Ont., November 1976.

Everding, H. Edward, Jr., and Dana W. Wilbanks. *Decision Making and the Bible.* Valley Forge, Pa.: Judson, 1975.

Everding, H. Edward, Jr., and Mary M. Wilcox. "Implications of Kohlberg's Theory of Moral Reasoning for Biblical Interpretation." Paper presented at the annual meeting of the Association of Professors and Researchers in Religious Education, Philadelphia, November 1975.

Felder, Cain Hope, ed. *Stony the Road We Trod: African American Biblical Interpretation.* Minneapolis: Fortress, 1991.

Ferguson, Marilyn. *The Aquarian Conspiracy: Personal and Social Transformation in the 1980s.* Los Angeles: Tarcher, 1980.

Foster, Charles R. *Educating Congregations: The Future of Christian Education.* Nashville: Abingdon, 1994.

Fowler, James W. *Becoming Adult, Becoming Christian: Adult Development and Christian Faith.* San Francisco: Harper & Row, 1984.

————. *Stages of Faith: The Psychology of Human Development and the Quest for Meaning.* San Francisco: Harper & Row, 1981.

Funk, Robert W. *Language, Hermeneutic, and Word of God: The Problem of Language in the New Testament and Contemporary Theology.* New York: Harper & Row, 1966.

Gilligan, Carol. *In a Different Voice: Psychological Theory and Women's Development.* Cambridge: Harvard University Press, 1982.

Goerner, Sally J. *Chaos and the Evolving Ecological Universe.* Amsterdam: Gordon & Breach, 1994.

Goldsmith, Joel S. *Consciousness Unfolding.* Secaucus, N.J.: Citadel, 1962.

Goodspeed, Edgar J. *The New Testament: An American Translation.* Chicago: University of Chicago Press, 1948.

"Green Atlas, The." *Mennonite,* January 20, 1980, 68ff.

Harris, Maria. *Fashion Me a People: Curriculum in the Church.* Louisville, Ky.: Westminster/John Knox, 1989.

Hatch, Nathan O., and Mark A. Noll, eds. *The Bible in America: Essays in Cultural History.* New York: Oxford University Press, 1982.

Inhelder, Bärbel, and Jean Piaget. *The Growth of Logical Thinking from Childhood to Adolescence.* New York: Basic, 1969.

Kohlberg, Lawrence. *Essays on Moral Development.* 2 vols. San Francisco: Harper & Row, 1981, 1984.

Kohlberg, Lawrence, Anne Colby, John Gibbs, and Betsy Speicher Dubin. *Standard Form Scoring Manual.* Pt. 3, *Form A Reference Manual.* Cambridge: Center for Moral Education, Harvard University, 1978.

Kuhn, Thomas S. *The Structure of Scientific Revolutions.* 2d ed. Chicago: University of Chicago Press, 1970.

Lee, James Michael. *Handbook of Faith.* Birmingham, Ala.: Religious Education Press, 1990.

Mead, Loren B. *The Once and Future Church: Reinventing the Congregation for a New Mission Frontier.* Bethesda, Md.: Alban Institute, 1991.

———. *Transforming Congregations for the Future.* Bethesda, Md.: Alban Institute, 1994.

Meyers, William. *Black and White Styles of Youth Ministry.* New York: Pilgrim, 1991.

Minnich, Elizabeth Kamarck. *Transforming Knowledge.* Philadelphia: Temple University Press, 1990.

Osmer, Richard Robert. *Teaching for Faith.* Louisville, Ky.: Westminster/John Knox, 1992.

Palmer, Parker J. *To Know as We Are Known: A Spirituality of Education.* San Francisco: Harper & Row, 1983.

Parks, Sharon. *The Critical Years: The Young Adult Search for a Faith to Live By.* San Francisco: Harper & Row, 1986.

Pelikan, Jaroslav. *Jesus through the Centuries: His Place in the History of Culture.* New Haven, Conn.: Yale University Press, 1985.

Perry, William G., Jr. *Forms of Intellectual and Ethical Development in the College Years.* New York: Holt, Rinehart & Winston, 1970.

Proudfoot, Wayne. *Religious Experience.* Berkeley: University of California Press, 1985.

Pulaski, Mary Ann Spencer. *Understanding Piaget: An Introduction to Children's Cognitive Development.* New York: Harper, 1971.

Rhoads, David. *The Challenge of Diversity: The Witness of Paul and the Gospels.* Minneapolis: Fortress, 1996.

Robinson, Wayne Bradley. *The Transforming Power of the Bible.* New York: Pilgrim, 1984.

Rowland, Christopher, and Mark Corner. *Liberating Exegesis: The Challenge of Liberation Theology to Biblical Studies.* Louisville, Ky.: Westminster/John Knox, 1989.

Russell, Keith A. *In Search of the Church: New Testament Images for Tomorrow's Congregations.* Bethesda, Md.: Alban Institute, 1994.

Russell, Letty M., ed. *Feminist Interpretation of the Bible.* Philadelphia: Westminster, 1985.

Samuels, Andrew. *The Plural Psyche.* London: Routledge, 1989.

Sanders, James A. *Canon and Community: A Guide to Canonical Criticism.* Philadelphia: Fortress, 1984.

Schottroff, Louise. *Let the Oppressed Go Free: Feminist Perspectives on the New Testament.* Louisville, Ky.: Westminster/John Knox, 1991.

Scott, Bernard Brandon. *Hear Then the Parable: A Commentary on the Parables of Jesus.* Minneapolis: Fortress, 1989.

Selman, Robert L. *The Growth of Interpersonal Understanding: Developmental and Clinical Analyses.* New York: Academic, 1980.

Seymour, Jack L., Margaret Ann Crain, and Joseph V. Crockett. *Educating Christians: The Intersection of Meaning, Learning, and Vocation.* Nashville: Abingdon, 1993.

Shepherd, Linda Jean. *Lifting the Veil: The Feminine Face of Science.* Boston: Shambhala, 1993.

Slater, Nelle, ed. *Tensions between Citizenship and Discipleship: A Case Study.* Cleveland: Pilgrim, 1989.

Snelling, Clarence H., Jr. Commencement address delivered at the graduation ceremony of the Iliff School of Theology, Denver, May 28, 1993.

———. "Symbolic Formation: A Structural-Developmental Study of Religious Language as Used by Theological Students." Presidential address given to the Association of Professors and Researchers in Religious Education, Hartford, Conn., October 1978.

———. "The Teaching Ministry: Four Types of Language." *Iliff Review* (spring 1966): 33–40.

Sugirtharajah, R. S., ed. *Voices from the Margin: Interpreting the Bible in the Third World.* Maryknoll, N.Y.: Orbis, 1991.

Talbot, Michael. *The Holographic Universe.* New York: HarperPerennial, 1991.

Tinker, George E. *Missionary Conquest: The Gospel and Native American Cultural Genocide.* Minneapolis: Fortress, 1993.

Tracy, David. *The Analogical Imagination: Christian Theology and the Culture of Pluralism.* New York: Crossroad, 1981.

Troeger, Thomas H. *The Parable of Ten Preachers.* Nashville: Abingdon, 1992.

Ward, Richard F. "The Listener as Active Participant." In *Speaking from the Heart: Preaching with Passion.* Nashville: Abingdon, 1992.

Watzlawick, Paul. *The Invented Reality: How Do We Know What We Believe We Know? Contributions to Constructivism.* New York: Norton, 1984.

Westerhoff, John H., III. *Living the Faith Community: The Church That Makes a Difference.* Minneapolis: Winston, 1985.

White, Benton. *Taking the Bible Seriously: Honest Differences about Biblical Interpretation.* Louisville, Ky.: Westminster/John Knox, 1993.

Wilcox, Mary M. *Developmental Journey: A Guide to the Development of Logical and Moral Reasoning and Social Perspective.* Nashville: Abingdon, 1979.

Wilcox, Mary M., and H. Edward Everding Jr. "The Boss Doesn't Get in Trouble." *JED SHARE* (August 1975): 5–6.

Wilcox, Mary M., H. Edward Everding Jr., and Clarence H. Snelling Jr. "Interpretation and Truth in Adult Development." Paper presented at the annual meeting of the Association of Professors and Researchers in Religious Education, Toronto, Ont., November 1979.

Wilder, Amos N. *Early Christian Rhetoric: The Language of the Gospel.* Cambridge: Harvard University Press, 1964.

Wink, Walter. *Transforming Bible Study: A Leader's Guide.* Nashville: Abingdon, 1980.

Zukav, Gary. *The Seat of the Soul.* New York: Simon & Schuster, 1989.

Scripture Index

General Index